The Rape of the Lock and Other Poems

Alexander Pope

Canto I

What dire offence from am'rous causes springs,

What mighty contests rise from trivial things,

I sing — This verse to Caryl, Muse! is due:

This, ev'n Belinda may vouchsafe to view:

Slight is the subject, but not so the praise,

If She inspire, and He approve my lays.

Say what strange motive, Goddess! could compel

A well-bred Lord t' assault a gentle Belle?

O say what stranger cause, yet unexplor'd,

Could make a gentle Belle reject a Lord?

In tasks so bold, can little men engage,

And in soft bosoms dwells such mighty Rage?

Sol thro' white curtains shot a tim'rous ray,

And oped those eyes that must eclipse the day:

Now lap-dogs give themselves the rousing shake,

And sleepless lovers, just at twelve, awake:

Thrice rung the bell, the slipper knock'd the ground,

And the press'd watch return'd a silver sound.

Belinda still her downy pillow prest,

Her guardian Sylph prolong'd the balmy rest:

'Twas He had summon'd to her silent bed

The morning-dream that hover'd o'er her head;

A Youth more glitt'ring than a Birth-night Beau,

(That ev'n in slumber caus'd her cheek to glow)

Seem'd to her ear his winning lips to lay,

And thus in whispers said, or seem'd to say.

Fairest of mortals, thou distinguish'd care

Of thousand bright Inhabitants of Air!

If e'er one vision touch.'d thy infant thought,

Of all the Nurse and all the Priest have taught;

Of airy Elves by moonlight shadows seen,

The silver token, and the circled green,

Or virgins visited by Angel-pow'rs,

With golden crowns and wreaths of heav'nly flow'rs;

Hear and believe! thy own importance know,

Nor bound thy narrow views to things below.

Some secret truths, from learned pride conceal'd,

To Maids alone and Children are reveal'd:

What tho' no credit doubting Wits may give?

The Fair and Innocent shall still believe.

Know, then, unnumber'd Spirits round thee fly,

The light Militia of the lower sky:

These, tho' unseen, are ever on the wing,

Hang o'er the Box, and hover round the Ring.

Think what an equipage thou hast in Air,

And view with scorn two Pages and a Chair.

As now your own, our beings were of old,

And once inclos'd in Woman's beauteous mould;

Thence, by a soft transition, we repair

From earthly Vehicles to these of air.

Think not, when Woman's transient breath is fled

That all her vanities at once are dead;

Succeeding vanities she still regards,

And tho' she plays no more, o'erlooks the cards.

Her joy in gilded Chariots, when alive,

And love of Ombre, after death survive.

For when the Fair in all their pride expire,

To their first Elements their Souls retire:

The Sprites of fiery Termagants in Flame

Mount up, and take a Salamander's name.

Soft yielding minds to Water glide away,

And sip, with Nymphs, their elemental Tea.

The graver Prude sinks downward to a Gnome,

In search of mischief still on Earth to roam.

The light Coquettes in Sylphs aloft repair,

And sport and flutter in the fields of Air.

"Know further yet; whoever fair and chaste

Rejects mankind, is by some Sylph embrac'd:

For Spirits, freed from mortal laws, with ease

Assume what sexes and what shapes they please.

What guards the purity of melting Maids,

In courtly balls, and midnight masquerades,

Safe from the treach'rous friend, the daring spark,

The glance by day, the whisper in the dark,

When kind occasion prompts their warm desires,

When music softens, and when dancing fires?

'Tis but their Sylph, the wise Celestials know,

Tho' Honour is the word with Men below.

Some nymphs there are, too conscious of their face,

For life predestin'd to the Gnomes' embrace.

These swell their prospects and exalt their pride,

When offers are disdain'd, and love deny'd:

Then gay Ideas crowd the vacant brain,

While Peers, and Dukes, and all their sweeping train,

And Garters, Stars, and Coronets appear,

And in soft sounds, Your Grace salutes their ear.

'T is these that early taint the female soul,

Instruct the eyes of young Coquettes to roll,

Teach Infant-cheeks a bidden blush to know,

And little hearts to flutter at a Beau.

Oft, when the world imagine women stray,

The Sylphs thro' mystic mazes guide their way,

Thro' all the giddy circle they pursue,

And old impertinence expel by new.

What tender maid but must a victim fall

To one man's treat, but for another's ball?

When Florio speaks what virgin could withstand,

If gentle Damon did not squeeze her hand?

With varying vanities, from ev'ry part,

They shift the moving Toyshop of their heart;

Where wigs with wigs, with sword-knots sword-knots strive,

Beaux banish beaux, and coaches coaches drive.

This erring mortals Levity may call;

Oh blind to truth! the Sylphs contrive it all.

Of these am I, who thy protection claim,

A watchful sprite, and Ariel is my name.

Late, as I rang'd the crystal wilds of air,

In the clear Mirror of thy ruling Star

I saw, alas! some dread event impend,

Ere to the main this morning sun descend,

But heav'n reveals not what, or how, or where:

Warn'd by the Sylph, oh pious maid, beware!

This to disclose is all thy guardian can:

Beware of all, but most beware of Man!"

He said; when Shock, who thought she slept too long,

Leap'd up, and wak'd his mistress with his tongue.

'T was then, Belinda, if report say true,

Thy eyes first open'd on a Billet-doux;

Wounds, Charms, and Ardors were no sooner read,

But all the Vision vanish'd from thy head.

And now, unveil'd, the Toilet stands display'd,

Each silver Vase in mystic order laid.

First, rob'd in white, the Nymph intent adores,

With head uncover'd, the Cosmetic pow'rs.

A heav'nly image in the glass appears,

To that she bends, to that her eyes she rears;

Th' inferior Priestess, at her altar's side,

Trembling begins the sacred rites of Pride.

Unnumber'd treasures ope at once, and here

The various off'rings of the world appear;

From each she nicely culls with curious toil,

And decks the Goddess with the glitt'ring spoil.

This casket India's glowing gems unlocks,

And all Arabia breathes from yonder box.

The Tortoise here and Elephant unite,

Transformed to combs, the speckled, and the white.

Here files of pins extend their shining rows,

Puffs, Powders, Patches, Bibles, Billet-doux.

Now awful Beauty puts on all its arms;

The fair each moment rises in her charms,

Repairs her smiles, awakens ev'ry grace,

And calls forth all the wonders of her face;

Sees by degrees a purer blush arise,

And keener lightnings quicken in her eyes.

The busy Sylphs surround their darling care,

These set the head, and those divide the hair,

Some fold the sleeve, whilst others plait the gown:

And Betty's prais'd for labours not her own.

5

10

15

20

25

30

.

35

40

45

50

55

60

65

70

75

80

85

90

95

100

105

110

115

120

125

130

135

140

145

Canto II

Not with more glories, in th' etherial plain,

The Sun first rises o'er the purpled main,

Than, issuing forth, the rival of his beams

Launch'd on the bosom of the silver Thames.

Fair Nymphs, and well-drest Youths around her shone.

But ev'ry eye was fix'd on her alone.

On her white breast a sparkling Cross she wore,

Which Jews might kiss, and Infidels adore.

Her lively looks a sprightly mind disclose,

Quick as her eyes, and as unfix'd as those:

Favours to none, to all she smiles extends;

Oft she rejects, but never once offends.

Bright as the sun, her eyes the gazers strike,

And, like the sun, they shine on all alike.

Yet graceful ease, and sweetness void of pride,

Might hide her faults, if Belles had faults to hide:

If to her share some female errors fall,

Look on her face, and you'll forget 'em all.

This Nymph, to the destruction of mankind,

Nourish'd two Locks, which graceful hung behind

In equal curls, and well conspir'd to deck

With shining ringlets the smooth iv'ry neck.

Love in these labyrinths his slaves detains,

And mighty hearts are held in slender chains.

With hairy springes we the birds betray,

Slight lines of hair surprise the finny prey,

Fair tresses man's imperial race ensnare,

And beauty draws us with a single hair.

Th' advent'rous Baron the bright locks admir'd;

He saw, he wish'd, and to the prize aspir'd.

Resolv'd to win, he meditates the way,

By force to ravish, or by fraud betray;

For when success a Lover's toil attends,

Few ask, if fraud or force attain'd his ends.

For this, ere Phœbus rose, he had implor'd

Propitious heav'n, and ev'ry pow'r ador'd,

But chiefly Love — to Love an Altar built,

Of twelve vast French Romances, neatly gilt.

There lay three garters, half a pair of gloves;

And all the trophies of his former loves;

With tender Billet-doux he lights the pyre,

And breathes three am'rous sighs to raise the fire.

Then prostrate falls, and begs with ardent eyes

Soon to obtain, and long possess the prize:

The pow'rs gave ear, and granted half his pray'r,

The rest, the winds dispers'd in empty air.

But now secure the painted vessel glides,

The sun-beams trembling on the floating tides:

While melting music steals upon the sky,

And soften'd sounds along the waters die;

Smooth flow the waves, the Zephyrs gently play,

Belinda smil'd, and all the world was gay.

All but the Sylph — with careful thoughts opprest,

Th' impending woe sat heavy on his breast.

He summons strait his Denizens of air;

The lucid squadrons round the sails repair:

Soft o'er the shrouds aërial whispers breathe,

That seem'd but Zephyrs to the train beneath.

Some to the sun their insect-wings unfold,

Waft on the breeze, or sink in clouds of gold;

Transparent forms, too fine for mortal sight,

Their fluid bodies half dissolv'd in light,

Loose to the wind their airy garments flew,

Thin glitt'ring textures of the filmy dew,

Dipt in the richest tincture of the skies,

Where light disports in ever-mingling dyes,

While ev'ry beam new transient colours flings,

Colours that change whene'er they wave their wings.

Amid the circle, on the gilded mast,

Superior by the head, was Ariel plac'd;

His purple pinions op'ning to the sun,

He rais'd his azure wand, and thus begun.

Ye Sylphs and Sylphids, to your chief give ear!

Fays, Fairies, Genii, Elves, and Dæmons, hear!

Ye know the spheres and various tasks assign'd

By laws eternal to th' aërial kind.

Some in the fields of purest Æther play,

And bask and whiten in the blaze of day.

Some guide the course of wand'ring orbs on high,

Or roll the planets thro' the boundless sky.

Some less refin'd, beneath the moon's pale light

Pursue the stars that shoot athwart the night,

Or suck the mists in grosser air below,

Or dip their pinions in the painted bow,

Or brew fierce tempests on the wintry main,

Or o'er the glebe distil the kindly rain.

Others on earth o'er human race preside,

Watch all their ways, and all their actions guide:

Of these the chief the care of Nations own,

And guard with Arms divine the British Throne.

Our humbler province is to tend the Fair,

Not a less pleasing, tho' less glorious care;

To save the powder from too rude a gale,

Nor let th' imprison'd-essences exhale;

To draw fresh colours from the vernal flow'rs;

To steal from rainbows e'er they drop in show'rs

A brighter wash; to curl their waving hairs,

Assist their blushes, and inspire their airs;

Nay oft, in dreams, invention we bestow,

To change a Flounce, or add a Furbelow.

This day, black Omens threat the brightest Fair,

That e'er deserv'd a watchful spirit's care;

Some dire disaster, or by force, or slight;

But what, or where, the fates have wrapt in night.

Whether the nymph shall break Diana's law,

Or some frail China jar receive a flaw;

Or stain her honour or her new brocade;

Forget her pray'rs, or miss a masquerade;

Or lose her heart, or necklace, at a ball;

Or whether Heav'n has doom'd that Shock must fall.

Haste, then, ye spirits! to your charge repair:

The flutt'ring fan be Zephyretta's care;

The drops to thee, Brillante, we consign;

And, Momentilla, let the watch be thine;

Do thou, Crispissa, tend her fav'rite Lock;

Ariel himself shall be the guard of Shock.

To fifty chosen Sylphs, of special note,

We trust th' important charge, the Petticoat:

Oft have we known that seven-fold fence to fail,

Tho' stiff with hoops, and arm'd with ribs of whale;

Form a strong line about the silver bound,

And guard the wide circumference around.

Whatever spirit, careless of his charge,

His post neglects, or leaves the fair at large,

Shall feel sharp vengeance soon o'ertake his sins,

Be stopp'd in vials, or transfix'd with pins;

Or plung'd in lakes of bitter washes lie,

Or wedg'd whole ages in a bodkin's eye:

Gums and Pomatums shall his flight restrain,

While clogg'd he beats his silken wings in vain;

Or Alum styptics with contracting pow'r

Shrink his thin essence like a rivel'd flow'r:

Or, as Ixion fix'd, the wretch shall feel

The giddy motion of the whirling Mill,

In fumes of burning Chocolate shall glow,

And tremble at the sea that froths below!

He spoke; the spirits from the sails descend;

Some, orb in orb, around the nymph extend;

Some thrid the mazy ringlets of her hair;

Some hang upon the pendants of her ear:

With beating hearts the dire event they wait,

Anxious, and trembling for the birth of Fate.

5

10

15

20

25

30

35

40

45

50

55

60

65

70

75

80

85

90

95

100

105

110

115

120

125

130

135

140

.

Canto III

Close by those meads, for ever crown'd with flow'rs,

Where Thames with pride surveys his rising tow'rs,

There stands a structure of majestic frame,

Which from the neighb'ring Hampton takes its name.

Here Britain's statesmen oft the fall foredoom

Of foreign Tyrants and of Nymphs at home;

Here thou, great Anna! whom three realms obey.

Dost sometimes counsel take — and sometimes Tea.

Hither the heroes and the nymphs resort,

To taste awhile the pleasures of a Court;

In various talk th' instructive hours they past,

Who gave the ball, or paid the visit last;

One speaks the glory of the British Queen,

And one describes a charming Indian screen;

A third interprets motions, looks, and eyes;

At ev'ry word a reputation dies.

Snuff, or the fan, supply each pause of chat,

With singing, laughing, ogling, and all that.

Mean while, declining from the noon of day,

The sun obliquely shoots his burning ray;

The hungry Judges soon the sentence sign,

And wretches hang that jury-men may dine;

The merchant from th' Exchange returns in peace,

And the long labours of the Toilet cease.

Belinda now, whom thirst of fame invites,

Burns to encounter two advent'rous Knights,

At Ombre singly to decide their doom;

And swells her breast with conquests yet to come.

Straight the three bands prepare in arms to join,

Each band the number of the sacred nine.

Soon as she spreads her hand, th' aërial guard

Descend, and sit on each important card:

First Ariel perch'd upon a Matadore,

Then each, according to the rank they bore;

For Sylphs, yet mindful of their ancient race,

Are, as when women, wondrous fond of place.

Behold, four Kings in majesty rever'd,

With hoary whiskers and a forky beard;

And four fair Queens whose hands sustain a flow'r,

Th' expressive emblem of their softer pow'r;

Four Knaves in garbs succinct, a trusty band,

Caps on their heads, and halberts in their hand;

And particolour'd troops, a shining train,

Draw forth to combat on the velvet plain.

The skilful Nymph reviews her force with care:

Let Spades be trumps! she said, and trumps they were.

Now move to war her sable Matadores,

In show like leaders of the swarthy Moors.

Spadillio first, unconquerable Lord!

Led off two captive trumps, and swept the board.

As many more Manillio forc'd to yield,

And march'd a victor from the verdant field.

Him Basto follow'd, but his fate more hard

Gain'd but one trump and one Plebeian card.

With his broad sabre next, a chief in years,

The hoary Majesty of Spades appears,

Puts forth one manly leg, to sight reveal'd,

The rest, his many-colour'd robe conceal'd.

The rebel Knave, who dares his prince engage,

Proves the just victim of his royal rage.

Ev'n mighty Pam, that Kings and Queens o'erthrew

And mow'd down armies in the fights of Lu,

Sad chance of war! now destitute of aid,

Falls undistinguish'd by the victor spade!

Thus far both armies to Belinda yield;

Now to the Baron fate inclines the field.

His warlike Amazon her host invades,

Th' imperial consort of the crown of Spades.

The Club's black Tyrant first her victim dy'd,

Spite of his haughty mien, and barb'rous pride:

What boots the regal circle on his head,

His giant limbs, in state unwieldy spread;

That long behind he trails his pompous robe,

And, of all monarchs, only grasps the globe?

The Baron now his Diamonds pours apace;

Th' embroider'd King who shows but half his face,

And his refulgent Queen, with pow'rs combin'd

Of broken troops an easy conquest find.

Clubs, Diamonds, Hearts, in wild disorder seen,

With throngs promiscuous strow the level green.

Thus when dispers'd a routed army runs,

Of Asia's troops, and Afric's sable sons,

With like confusion different nations fly,

Of various habit, and of various dye,

The pierc'd battalions dis-united fall,

In heaps on heaps; one fate o'erwhelms them all.

The Knave of Diamonds tries his wily arts,

And wins (oh shameful chance!) the Queen of Hearts.

At this, the blood the virgin's cheek forsook,

A livid paleness spreads o'er all her look;

She sees, and trembles at th' approaching ill,

Just in the jaws of ruin, and Codille.

And now (as oft in some distemper'd State)

On one nice Trick depends the gen'ral fate.

An Ace of Hearts steps forth: The King unseen

Lurk'd in her hand, and mourn'd his captive Queen:

He springs to Vengeance with an eager pace,

And falls like thunder on the prostrate Ace.

The nymph exulting fills with shouts the sky;

The walls, the woods, and long canals reply.

Oh thoughtless mortals! ever blind to fate,

Too soon dejected, and too soon elate.

Sudden, these honours shall be snatch'd away,

And curs'd for ever this victorious day.

For lo! the board with cups and spoons is crown'd,

The berries crackle, and the mill turns round;

On shining Altars of Japan they raise

The silver lamp; the fiery spirits blaze:

From silver spouts the grateful liquors glide,

While China's earth receives the smoking tide:

At once they gratify their scent and taste,

And frequent cups prolong the rich repast.

Straight hover round the Fair her airy band;

Some, as she sipp'd, the fuming liquor fann'd,

Some o'er her lap their careful plumes display'd,

Trembling, and conscious of the rich brocade.

Coffee, (which makes the politician wise,

And see thro' all things with his half-shut eyes)

Sent up in vapours to the Baron's brain

New Stratagems, the radiant Lock to gain.

Ah cease, rash youth! desist ere't is too late,

Fear the just Gods, and think of Scylla's Fate!

Chang'd to a bird, and sent to flit in air,

She dearly pays for Nisus' injur'd hair!

But when to mischief mortals bend their will,

How soon they find fit instruments of ill!

Just then, Clarissa drew with tempting grace

A two-edg'd weapon from her shining case:

So Ladies in Romance assist their Knight,

Present the spear, and arm him for the fight.

He takes the gift with rev'rence, and extends

The little engine on his fingers' ends;

This just behind Belinda's neck he spread,

As o'er the fragrant steams she bends her head.

Swift to the Lock a thousand Sprites repair,

A thousand wings, by turns, blow back the hair;

And thrice they twitch'd the diamond in her ear;

Thrice she look'd back, and thrice the foe drew near.

Just in that instant, anxious Ariel sought

The close recesses of the Virgin's thought;

As on the nosegay in her breast reclin'd,

He watch'd th' Ideas rising in her mind,

Sudden he view'd, in spite of all her art,

An earthly Lover lurking at her heart.

Amaz'd, confus'd, he found his pow'r expir'd,

Resign'd to fate, and with a sigh retir'd.

The Peer now spreads the glitt'ring Forfex wide,

T' inclose the Lock; now joins it, to divide.

Ev'n then, before the fatal engine clos'd,

A wretched Sylph too fondly interpos'd;

Fate urg'd the shears, and cut the Sylph in twain,

(But airy substance soon unites again)

The meeting points the sacred hair dissever

From the fair head, for ever, and for ever!

Then flash'd the living lightning from her eyes,

And screams of horror rend th' affrighted skies.

Not louder shrieks to pitying heav'n are cast,

When husbands, or when lapdogs breathe their last;

Or when rich China vessels fall'n from high,

In glitt'ring dust and painted fragments lie!

Let wreaths of triumph now my temples twine

(The victor cry'd) the glorious Prize is mine!

While fish in streams, or birds delight in air,

Or in a coach and six the British Fair,

As long as Atalantis shall be read,

Or the small pillow grace a Lady's bed,

While visits shall be paid on solemn days,

When num'rous wax-lights in bright order blaze,

While nymphs take treats, or assignations give,

So long my honour, name, and praise shall live!

What Time would spare, from Steel receives its date,

And monuments, like men, submit to fate!

Steel could the labour of the Gods destroy,

And strike to dust th' imperial tow'rs of Troy;

Steel could the works of mortal pride confound,

And hew triumphal arches to the ground.

What wonder then, fair nymph! thy hairs should feel,

The conqu'ring force of unresisted steel?

5

10

15

20

25

30

35

40

45

50

55

60

65

70

75

80

85

90

95

100

105

110

115

120

125

130

135

140

145

150

155

160

165

170

175

Canto IV

But anxious cares the pensive nymph oppress'd,

And secret passions labour'd in her breast.

Not youthful kings in battle seiz'd alive,

Not scornful virgins who their charms survive,

Not ardent lovers robb'd of all their bliss,

Not ancient ladies when refus'd a kiss,

Not tyrants fierce that unrepenting die,

Not Cynthia when her manteau's pinn'd awry,

E'er felt such rage, resentment, and despair,

As thou, sad Virgin! for thy ravish'd Hair.

For, that sad moment, when the Sylphs withdrew

And Ariel weeping from Belinda flew,

Umbriel, a dusky, melancholy sprite,

As ever sully'd the fair face of light,

Down to the central earth, his proper scene,

Repair'd to search the gloomy Cave of Spleen.

Swift on his sooty pinions flits the Gnome,

And in a vapour reach'd the dismal dome.

No cheerful breeze this sullen region knows,

The dreaded East is all the wind that blows.

Here in a grotto, shelter'd close from air,

And screen'd in shades from day's detested glare,

She sighs for ever on her pensive bed,

Pain at her side, and Megrim at her head.

Two handmaids wait the throne: alike in place,

But diff'ring far in figure and in face.

Here stood Ill-nature like an ancient maid,

Her wrinkled form in black and white array'd;

With store of pray'rs, for mornings, nights, and noons,

Her hand is fill'd; her bosom with lampoons.

There Affectation, with a sickly mien,

Shows in her cheek the roses of eighteen,

Practis'd to lisp, and hang the head aside.

Faints into airs, and languishes with pride,

On the rich quilt sinks with becoming woe,

Wrapt in a gown, for sickness, and for show.

The fair ones feel such maladies as these,

When each new night-dress gives a new disease.

A constant Vapour o'er the palace flies;

Strange phantoms rising as the mists arise;

Dreadful, as hermit's dreams in haunted shades,

Or bright, as visions of expiring maids.

Now glaring fiends, and snakes on rolling spires,

Pale spectres, gaping tombs, and purple fires:

Now lakes of liquid gold, Elysian scenes,

And crystal domes, and angels in machines.

Unnumber'd throngs on every side are seen,

Of bodies chang'd to various forms by Spleen.

Here living Tea-pots stand, one arm held out,

One bent; the handle this, and that the spout:

A Pipkin there, like Homer's Tripod walks;

Here sighs a Jar, and there a Goose-pie talks;

Men prove with child, as pow'rful fancy works,

And maids turn'd bottles, call aloud for corks.

Safe past the Gnome thro' this fantastic band,

A branch of healing Spleenwort in his hand.

Then thus address'd the pow'r: "Hail, wayward Queen!

Who rule the sex to fifty from fifteen:

Parent of vapours and of female wit,

Who give th' hysteric, or poetic fit,

On various tempers act by various ways,

Make some take physic, others scribble plays;

Who cause the proud their visits to delay,

And send the godly in a pet to pray.

A nymph there is, that all thy pow'r disdains,

And thousands more in equal mirth maintains.

But oh! if e'er thy Gnome could spoil a grace,

Or raise a pimple on a beauteous face,

Like Citron-waters matrons cheeks inflame,

Or change complexions at a losing game;

If e'er with airy horns I planted heads,

Or rumpled petticoats, or tumbled beds,

Or caus'd suspicion when no soul was rude,

Or discompos'd the head-dress of a Prude,

Or e'er to costive lap-dog gave disease,

Which not the tears of brightest eyes could ease:

Hear me, and touch Belinda with chagrin,

That single act gives half the world the spleen."

The Goddess with a discontented air

Seems to reject him, tho' she grants his pray'r.

A wond'rous Bag with both her hands she binds,

Like that where once Ulysses held the winds;

There she collects the force of female lungs,

Sighs, sobs, and passions, and the war of tongues.

A Vial next she fills with fainting fears,

Soft sorrows, melting griefs, and flowing tears.

The Gnome rejoicing bears her gifts away,

Spreads his black wings, and slowly mounts to day.

Sunk in Thalestris' arms the nymph he found,

Her eyes dejected and her hair unbound.

Full o'er their heads the swelling bag he rent,

And all the Furies issu'd at the vent.

Belinda burns with more than mortal ire,

And fierce Thalestris fans the rising fire.

"O wretched maid!" she spread her hands, and cry'd,

(While Hampton's echoes, "Wretched maid!" reply'd)

"Was it for this you took such constant care

The bodkin, comb, and essence to prepare?

For this your locks in paper durance bound,

For this with tort'ring irons wreath'd around?

For this with fillets strain'd your tender head,

And bravely bore the double loads of lead?

Gods! shall the ravisher display your hair,

While the Fops envy, and the Ladies stare!

Honour forbid! at whose unrivall'd shrine

Ease, pleasure, virtue, all our sex resign.

Methinks already I your tears survey,

Already hear the horrid things they say,

Already see you a degraded toast,

And all your honour in a whisper lost!

How shall I, then, your helpless fame defend?

'T will then be infamy to seem your friend!

And shall this prize, th' inestimable prize,

Expos'd thro' crystal to the gazing eyes,

And heighten'd by the diamond's circling rays,

On that rapacious hand for ever blaze?

Sooner shall grass in Hyde-park Circus grow,

And wits take lodgings in the sound of Bow;

Sooner let earth, air, sea, to Chaos fall,

Men, monkeys, lap-dogs, parrots, perish all!"

She said; then raging to Sir Plume repairs,

And bids her Beau demand the precious hairs;

(Sir Plume of amber snuff-box justly vain,

And the nice conduct of a clouded cane)

With earnest eyes, and round unthinking face,

He first the snuff-box open'd, then the case,

And thus broke out — "My Lord, why, what the devil?

"Z — ds! damn the lock! 'fore Gad, you must be civil!

Plague on't!'t is past a jest — nay prithee, pox!

Give her the hair" — he spoke, and rapp'd his box.

"It grieves me much" (reply'd the Peer again)

"Who speaks so well should ever speak in vain.

But by this Lock, this sacred Lock I swear,

(Which never more shall join its parted hair;

Which never more its honours shall renew,

Clipp'd from the lovely head where late it grew)

That while my nostrils draw the vital air,

This hand, which won it, shall for ever wear."

He spoke, and speaking, in proud triumph spread

The long-contended honours of her head.

But Umbriel, hateful Gnome! forbears not so;

He breaks the Vial whence the sorrows flow.

Then see! the nymph in beauteous grief appears,

Her eyes half-languishing, half-drown'd in tears;

On her heav'd bosom hung her drooping head,

Which, with a sigh, she rais'd; and thus she said.

"For ever curs'd be this detested day,

Which snatch'd my best, my fav'rite curl away!

Happy! ah ten times happy had I been,

If Hampton-Court these eyes had never seen!

Yet am not I the first mistaken maid,

By love of Courts to num'rous ills betray'd.

Oh had I rather un-admir'd remain'd

In some lone isle, or distant Northern land;

Where the gilt Chariot never marks the way,

Where none learn Ombre, none e'er taste Bohea!

There kept my charms conceal'd from mortal eye,

Like roses, that in deserts bloom and die.

What mov'd my mind with youthful Lords to roam?

Oh had I stay'd, and said my pray'rs at home!

'T was this, the morning omens seem'd to tell,

Thrice from my trembling hand the patch-box fell;

The tott'ring China shook without a wind.

Nay, Poll sat mute, and Shock was most unkind!

A Sylph too warn'd me of the threats of fate,

In mystic visions, now believ'd too late!

See the poor remnants of these slighted hairs!

My hands shall rend what ev'n thy rapine spares:

These in two sable ringlets taught to break,

Once gave new beauties to the snowy neck;

The sister-lock now sits uncouth, alone,

And in its fellow's fate foresees its own;

Uncurl'd it hangs, the fatal shears demands,

And tempts once more thy sacrilegious hands.

Oh hadst thou, cruel! been content to seize

Hairs less in sight, or any hairs but these!"

5

10

15

20

25

30

35

40

45

50

55

60

65

70

75

80

85

90

95

100

105

110

115

120

125

130

135

140

145

150

155

160

165

170

175

Canto V

She said: the pitying audience melt in tears.

But Fate and Jove had stopp'd the Baron's ears.

In vain Thalestris with reproach assails,

For who can move when fair Belinda fails?

Not half so fix'd the Trojan could remain,

While Anna begg'd and Dido rag'd in vain.

Then grave Clarissa graceful wav'd her fan;

Silence ensu'd, and thus the nymph began.

"Say why are Beauties prais'd and honour'd most,

The wise man's passion, and the vain man's toast?

Why deck'd with all that land and sea afford,

Why Angels call'd, and Angel-like ador'd?

Why round our coaches crowd the white-glov'd Beaux,

Why bows the side-box from its inmost rows;

How vain are all these glories, all our pains,

Unless good sense preserve what beauty gains:

That men may say, when we the front-box grace:

'Behold the first in virtue as in face!'

Oh! if to dance all night, and dress all day,

Charm'd the small-pox, or chas'd old-age away;

Who would not scorn what housewife's cares produce,

Or who would learn one earthly thing of use?

To patch, nay ogle, might become a Saint,

Nor could it sure be such a sin to paint.

But since, alas! frail beauty must decay,

Curl'd or uncurl'd, since Locks will turn to grey;

Since painted, or not painted, all shall fade,

And she who scorns a man, must die a maid;

What then remains but well our pow'r to use,

And keep good-humour still whate'er we lose?

And trust me, dear! good-humour can prevail,

When airs, and flights, and screams, and scolding fail.

Beauties in vain their pretty eyes may roll;

Charms strike the sight, but merit wins the soul."

So spoke the Dame, but no applause ensu'd;

Belinda frown'd, Thalestris call'd her Prude.

"To arms, to arms!" the fierce Virago cries,

And swift as lightning to the combat flies.

All side in parties, and begin th' attack;

Fans clap, silks rustle, and tough whalebones crack;

Heroes' and Heroines' shouts confus'dly rise,

And bass, and treble voices strike the skies.

No common weapons in their hands are found,

Like Gods they fight, nor dread a mortal wound.

So when bold Homer makes the Gods engage,

And heav'nly breasts with human passions rage;

'Gainst Pallas, Mars; Latona, Hermes arms;

And all Olympus rings with loud alarms:

Jove's thunder roars, heav'n trembles all around,

Blue Neptune storms, the bellowing deeps resound:

Earth shakes her nodding tow'rs, the ground gives way.

And the pale ghosts start at the flash of day!

Triumphant Umbriel on a sconce's height

Clapp'd his glad wings, and sate to view the fight:

Propp'd on the bodkin spears, the Sprites survey

The growing combat, or assist the fray.

While thro' the press enrag'd Thalestris flies,

And scatters death around from both her eyes,

A Beau and Witling perish'd in the throng,

One died in metaphor, and one in song.

"O cruel nymph! a living death I bear,"

Cry'd Dapperwit, and sunk beside his chair.

A mournful glance Sir Fopling upwards cast,

"Those eyes are made so killing" — was his last.

Thus on Mæander's flow'ry margin lies

Th' expiring Swan, and as he sings he dies.

When bold Sir Plume had drawn Clarissa down,

Chloe stepp'd in, and kill'd him with a frown;

She smil'd to see the doughty hero slain,

But, at her smile, the Beau reviv'd again.

Now Jove suspends his golden scales in air,

Weighs the Men's wits against the Lady's hair;

The doubtful beam long nods from side to side;

At length the wits mount up, the hairs subside.

See, fierce Belinda on the Baron flies,

With more than usual lightning in her eyes:

Nor fear'd the Chief th' unequal fight to try,

Who sought no more than on his foe to die.

But this bold Lord with manly strength endu'd,

She with one finger and a thumb subdu'd:

Just where the breath of life his nostrils drew,

A charge of Snuff the wily virgin threw;

The Gnomes direct, to ev'ry atom just,

The pungent grains of titillating dust.

Sudden, with starting tears each eye o'erflows,

And the high dome re-echoes to his nose.

Now meet thy fate, incens'd Belinda cry'd,

And drew a deadly bodkin from her side.

(The same, his ancient personage to deck,

Her great great grandsire wore about his neck,

In three seal-rings; which after, melted down,

Form'd a vast buckle for his widow's gown:

Her infant grandame's whistle next it grew,

The bells she jingled, and the whistle blew;

Then in a bodkin grac'd her mother's hairs,

Which long she wore, and now Belinda wears.)

"Boast not my fall" (he cry'd) "insulting foe!

Thou by some other shalt be laid as low,

Nor think, to die dejects my lofty mind:

All that I dread is leaving you behind!

Rather than so, ah let me still survive,

And burn in Cupid's flames — but burn alive."

"Restore the Lock!" she cries; and all around

"Restore the Lock!" the vaulted roofs rebound.

Not fierce Othello in so loud a strain

Roar'd for the handkerchief that caus'd his pain.

But see how oft ambitious aims are cross'd,

And chiefs contend 'till all the prize is lost!

The Lock, obtain'd with guilt, and kept with pain,

In ev'ry place is sought, but sought in vain:

With such a prize no mortal must be blest,

So heav'n decrees! with heav'n who can contest?

Some thought it mounted to the Lunar sphere,

Since all things lost on earth are treasur'd there.

There Hero's wits are kept in pond'rous vases,

And beau's in snuff-boxes and tweezer-cases.

There broken vows and death-bed alms are found,

And lovers' hearts with ends of riband bound,

The courtier's promises, and sick man's pray'rs,

The smiles of harlots, and the tears of heirs,

Cages for gnats, and chains to yoke a flea,

Dry'd butterflies, and tomes of casuistry.

But trust the Muse — she saw it upward rise,

Tho' mark'd by none but quick, poetic eyes:

(So Rome's great founder to the heav'ns withdrew,

To Proculus alone confess'd in view)

A sudden Star, it shot thro' liquid air,

And drew behind a radiant trail of hair.

Not Berenice's Locks first rose so bright,

The heav'ns bespangling with dishevell'd light.

The Sylphs behold it kindling as it flies,

And pleas'd pursue its progress thro' the skies.

This the Beau monde shall from the Mall survey,

And hail with music its propitious ray.

This the blest Lover shall for Venus take,

And send up vows from Rosamonda's lake.

This Partridge soon shall view in cloudless skies,

When next he looks thro' Galileo's eyes;

And hence th' egregious wizard shall foredoom

The fate of Louis, and the fall of Rome.

Then cease, bright Nymph! to mourn thy ravish'd hair,

Which adds new glory to the shining sphere!

Not all the tresses that fair head can boast,

Shall draw such envy as the Lock you lost.

For, after all the murders of your eye,

When, after millions slain, yourself shall die:

When those fair suns shall set, as set they must,

And all those tresses shall be laid in dust,

This Lock, the Muse shall consecrate to fame,

And 'midst the stars inscribe Belinda's name.

5

10

15

20

25

30

35

40

45

50

55

60

65

70

75

80

85

90

95

100

105

110

115

120

125

130

135

140

145

150

Contents

An Essay on Criticism

Contents

Part	Line Topic
I	
Introduction	
	1 That 'tis

as great a fault to judge ill, as to write ill, and a more dangerous one to the public.

| | 9-18
That a |

true Taste is as rare to be found, as a true Genius.

| | 19-25
That |

most men are born with some Taste, but spoiled by false Education.

| | 26-45
The |

multitude of Critics, and causes of them.

| | 46-67
That we |

are to study our own Taste, and know the Limits of it.

| | 68-87
Nature |

the best guide of Judgment.

| | 88
Improv' |

d by Art and Rules, — which are but methodis'd Nature.

in Wit, Language, Versification, only.

er of a good Critic.

Roscommon, etc.

Conclusion

Contents

An Essay on Criticism

'Tis hard to say, if greater want of skill

Appear in writing or in judging ill;

But, of the two, less dang'rous is th' offence

To tire our patience, than mislead our sense.

Some few in that, but numbers err in this,

Ten censure wrong for one who writes amiss;

A fool might once himself alone expose,

Now one in verse makes many more in prose.

'Tis with our judgments as our watches, none

Go just alike, yet each believes his own.

In Poets as true genius is but rare,

True Taste as seldom is the Critic's share;

Both must alike from Heav'n derive their light,

These born to judge, as well as those to write.

Let such teach others who themselves excel,

And censure freely who have written well.

Authors are partial to their wit, 'tis true,

But are not Critics to their judgment too?

Yet if we look more closely, we shall find

Most have the seeds of judgment in their mind:

Nature affords at least a glimm'ring light;

The lines, tho' touch'd but faintly, are drawn right.

(But as the slightest sketch, if justly trac'd,

(Is by ill-colouring but the more disgrac'd,

(So by false learning is good sense defac'd:

Some are bewilder'd in the maze of schools,

And some made coxcombs Nature meant but fools.

In search of wit these lose their common sense,

And then turn Critics in their own defence:

Each burns alike, who can, or cannot write,

Or with a Rival's, or an Eunuch's spite.

All fools have still an itching to deride,

And fain would be upon the laughing side.

If Mævius scribble in Apollo's spite,

There are who judge still worse than he can write.

Some have at first for Wits, then Poets past,

Turn'd Critics next, and prov'd plain fools at last.

Some neither can for Wits nor Critics pass,

As heavy mules are neither horse nor ass.

Those half-learn'd witlings, num'rous in our isle,

As half-form'd insects on the banks of Nile;

Unfinish'd things, one knows not what to call,

Their generation's so equivocal:

To tell 'em, would a hundred tongues require,

Or one vain wit's, that might a hundred tire.

But you who seek to give and merit fame,

And justly bear a Critic's noble name,

Be sure yourself and your own reach to know,

How far your genius, taste, and learning go;

Launch not beyond your depth, but be discreet,

And mark that point where sense and dulness meet.

Nature to all things fix'd the limits fit,

And wisely curb'd proud man's pretending wit.

As on the land while here the ocean gains,

In other parts it leaves wide sandy plains;

Thus in the soul while memory prevails,

The solid pow'r of understanding fails;

Where beams of warm imagination play,

The memory's soft figures melt away.

One science only will one genius fit;

So vast is art, so narrow human wit:

Not only bounded to peculiar arts,

But oft in those confin'd to single parts.

Like kings we lose the conquests gain'd before,

By vain ambition still to make them more;

Each might his sev'ral province well command,

Would all but stoop to what they understand.

First follow Nature, and your judgment frame

By her just standard, which is still the same:

Unerring Nature, still divinely bright,

One clear, unchang'd, and universal light,

Life, force, and beauty, must to all impart,

At once the source, and end, and test of Art.

Art from that fund each just supply provides,

Works without show, and without pomp presides:

In some fair body thus th' informing soul

With spirits feeds, with vigour fills the whole,

Each motion guides, and ev'ry nerve sustains;

Itself unseen, but in th' effects, remains.

Some, to whom Heav'n in wit has been profuse,

Want as much more, to turn it to its use;

For wit and judgment often are at strife,

Tho' meant each other's aid, like man and wife.

'T is more to guide, than spur the Muse's steed;

Restrain his fury, than provoke his speed;

The winged courser, like a gen'rous horse,

Shows most true mettle when you check his course.

Those Rules of old discovered, not devis'd,

Are Nature still, but Nature methodiz'd;

Nature, like liberty, is but restrain'd

By the same laws which first herself ordain'd.

Hear how learn'd Greece her useful rules indites,

When to repress, and when indulge our flights:

High on Parnassus' top her sons she show'd,

And pointed out those arduous paths they trod;

Held from afar, aloft, th' immortal prize,

And urg'd the rest by equal steps to rise.

Just precepts thus from great examples giv'n,

She drew from them what they deriv'd from Heav'n.

The gen'rous Critic fann'd the Poet's fire,

And taught the world with reason to admire.

Then Criticism the Muse's handmaid prov'd,

To dress her charms, and make her more belov'd:

But following wits from that intention stray'd,

Who could not win the mistress, woo'd the maid;

Against the Poets their own arms they turn'd,

Sure to hate most the men from whom they learn'd.

So modern 'Pothecaries, taught the art

By Doctor's bills to play the Doctor's part,

Bold in the practice of mistaken rules,

Prescribe, apply, and call their masters fools.

Some on the leaves of ancient authors prey,

Nor time nor moths e'er spoil'd so much as they.

Some drily plain, without invention's aid,

Write dull receipts how poems may be made.

These leave the sense, their learning to display,

And those explain the meaning quite away.

You then whose judgment the right course would steer,

Know well each Ancient's proper character;

His fable, subject, scope in ev'ry page;

Religion, Country, genius of his Age:

Without all these at once before your eyes,

Cavil you may, but never criticize.

Be Homer's works your study and delight,

Read them by day, and meditate by night;

Thence form your judgment, thence your maxims bring,

And trace the Muses upward to their spring.

Still with itself compar'd, his text peruse;

And let your comment be the Mantuan Muse.

When first young Maro in his boundless mind

A work t' outlast immortal Rome design'd,

Perhaps he seem'd above the critic's law,

And but from Nature's fountains scorn'd to draw:

But when t' examine ev'ry part he came,

Nature and Homer were, he found, the same.

Convinc'd, amaz'd, he checks the bold design;

And rules as strict his labour'd work confine,

As if the Stagirite o'erlook'd each line.

Learn hence for ancient rules a just esteem;

To copy nature is to copy them.

Some beauties yet no Precepts can declare,

For there's a happiness as well as care.

Music resembles Poetry, in each

Are nameless graces which no methods teach,

And which a master-hand alone can reach.

If, where the rules not far enough extend,

(Since rules were made but to promote their end)

Some lucky Licence answer to the full

Th' intent propos'd, that Licence is a rule.

Thus Pegasus, a nearer way to take,

May boldly deviate from the common track;

From vulgar bounds with brave disorder part,

And snatch a grace beyond the reach of art,

Which without passing thro' the judgment, gains

The heart, and all its end at once attains.

In prospects thus, some objects please our eyes,

Which out of nature's common order rise,

The shapeless rock, or hanging precipice.

Great wits sometimes may gloriously offend,

And rise to faults true Critics dare not mend.

But tho' the Ancients thus their rules invade,

(As Kings dispense with laws themselves have made)

Moderns, beware! or if you must offend

Against the precept, ne'er transgress its End;

Let it be seldom, and compell'd by need;

And have, at least, their precedent to plead.

The Critic else proceeds without remorse,

Seizes your fame, and puts his laws in force.

I know there are, to whose presumptuous thoughts

Those freer beauties, ev'n in them, seem faults.

Some figures monstrous and mis-shap'd appear,

Consider'd singly, or beheld too near,

Which, but proportion'd to their light, or place,

Due distance reconciles to form and grace.

A prudent chief not always must display

His pow'rs in equal ranks, and fair array.

But with th' occasion and the place comply,

Conceal his force, nay seem sometimes to fly.

Those oft are stratagems which error seem,

Nor is it Homer nods, but we that dream.

Still green with bays each ancient Altar stands,

Above the reach of sacrilegious hands;

Secure from Flames, from Envy's fiercer rage,

Destructive War, and all-involving Age.

See, from each clime the learn'd their incense bring!

Hear, in all tongues consenting Pæans ring!

In praise so just let ev'ry voice be join'd,

And fill the gen'ral chorus of mankind.

Hail, Bards triumphant! born in happier days;

Immortal heirs of universal praise!

Whose honours with increase of ages grow,

As streams roll down, enlarging as they flow;

Nations unborn your mighty names shall sound,

And worlds applaud that must not yet be found!

Oh may some spark of your celestial fire,

The last, the meanest of your sons inspire,

(That on weak wings, from far, pursues your flights;

Glows while he reads, but trembles as he writes)

To teach vain Wits a science little known,

T' admire superior sense, and doubt their own!

Of all the Causes which conspire to blind

Man's erring judgment, and misguide the mind,

What the weak head with strongest bias rules,

Is Pride, the never-failing voice of fools.

Whatever nature has in worth denied,

She gives in large recruits of needful pride;

For as in bodies, thus in souls, we find

What wants in blood and spirits, swell'd with wind:

Pride, where wit fails, steps in to our defence,

And fills up all the mighty Void of sense.

If once right reason drives that cloud away,

Truth breaks upon us with resistless day.

Trust not yourself; but your defects to know,

Make use of ev'ry friend — and ev'ry foe.

A little learning is a dang'rous thing;

Drink deep, or taste not the Pierian spring.

There shallow draughts intoxicate the brain,

And drinking largely sobers us again.

Fir'd at first sight with what the Muse imparts,

In fearless youth we tempt the heights of Arts,

While from the bounded level of our mind

Short views we take, nor see the lengths behind;

But more advanc'd, behold with strange surprise

New distant scenes of endless science rise!

So pleas'd at first the tow'ring Alps we try,

Mount o'er the vales, and seem to tread the sky,

Th' eternal snows appear already past,

And the first clouds and mountains seem the last;

c

But, those attain'd, we tremble to survey

The growing labours of the lengthen'd way,

Th' increasing prospect tires our wand'ring eyes,

Hills peep o'er hills, and Alps on Alps arise!

A perfect Judge will read each work of Wit

With the same spirit that its author writ:

Survey the Whole, nor seek slight faults to find

Where nature moves, and rapture warms the mind;

Nor lose, for that malignant dull delight,

The gen'rous pleasure to be charm'd with Wit.

But in such lays as neither ebb, nor flow,

Correctly cold, and regularly low,

That shunning faults, one quiet tenour keep,

We cannot blame indeed — but we may sleep.

In wit, as nature, what affects our hearts

Is not th' exactness of peculiar parts;

'Tis not a lip, or eye, we beauty call,

But the joint force and full result of all.

Thus when we view some well-proportion'd dome,

(The world's just wonder, and ev'n thine, O Rome!)

No single parts unequally surprize,

All comes united to th' admiring eyes;

No monstrous height, or breadth, or length appear;

The Whole at once is bold, and regular.

Whoever thinks a faultless piece to see,

Thinks what ne'er was, nor is, nor e'er shall be.

In every work regard the writer's End,

Since none can compass more than they intend;

And if the means be just, the conduct true,

Applause, in spight of trivial faults, is due;

As men of breeding, sometimes men of wit,

T' avoid great errors, must the less commit:

Neglect the rules each verbal Critic lays,

For not to know some trifles, is a praise.

Most Critics, fond of some subservient art,

Still make the Whole depend upon a Part:

They talk of principles, but notions prize,

And all to one lov'd Folly sacrifice.

Once on a time, La Mancha's Knight, they say,

A certain bard encount'ring on the way,

Discours'd in terms as just, with looks as sage,

As e'er could Dennis of the Grecian stage;

Concluding all were desp'rate sots and fools,

Who durst depart from Aristotle's rules.

Our Author, happy in a judge so nice,

Produc'd his Play, and begg'd the Knight's advice;

Made him observe the subject, and the plot,

The manners, passions, unities; what not?

All which, exact to rule, were brought about,

Were but a Combat in the lists left out.

"What! leave the Combat out?" exclaims the Knight;

Yes, or we must renounce the Stagirite.

"Not so, by Heav'n" (he answers in a rage),

"Knights, squires, and steeds, must enter on the stage."

So vast a throng the stage can ne'er contain.

"Then build a new, or act it in a plain."

Thus Critics, of less judgment than caprice,

Curious not knowing, not exact but nice,

Form short Ideas; and offend in arts

(As most in manners) by a love to parts.

Some to Conceit alone their taste confine,

And glitt'ring thoughts struck out at ev'ry line;

Pleas'd with a work where nothing's just or fit;

One glaring Chaos and wild heap of wit.

Poets like painters, thus, unskill'd to trace

The naked nature and the living grace,

With gold and jewels cover ev'ry part,

And hide with ornaments their want of art.

True Wit is Nature to advantage dress'd,

What oft was thought, but ne'er so well express'd;

Something, whose truth convinc'd at sight we find,

That gives us back the image of our mind.

As shades more sweetly recommend the light,

So modest plainness sets off sprightly wit.

For works may have more wit than does 'em good,

As bodies perish thro' excess of blood.

Others for Language all their care express,

And value books, as women men, for Dress:

Their praise is still — the Style is excellent:

The Sense, they humbly take upon content.

Words are like leaves; and where they most abound,

Much fruit of sense beneath is rarely found,

False Eloquence, like the prismatic glass,

Its gaudy colours spreads on ev'ry place;

The face of Nature we no more survey,

All glares alike, without distinction gay:

But true expression, like th' unchanging Sun,

Clears and improves whate'er it shines upon,

It gilds all objects, but it alters none.

Expression is the dress of thought, and still

Appears more decent, as more suitable;

A vile conceit in pompous words express'd,

Is like a clown in regal purple dress'd:

For diff'rent styles with diff'rent subjects sort,

As several garbs with country, town, and court.

Some by old words to fame have made pretence,

Ancients in phrase, mere moderns in their sense;

Such labour'd nothings, in so strange a style,

Amaze th' unlearn'd, and make the learned smile.

(Unlucky, as Fungoso in the play,

(These sparks with awkward vanity display

(What the fine gentleman wore yesterday;

And but so mimic ancient wits at best,

As apes our grandsires, in their doublets drest.

In words, as fashions, the same rule will hold;

Alike fantastic, if too new, or old:

Be not the first by whom the new are try'd,

Nor yet the last to lay the old aside.

But most by Numbers judge a Poet's song;

And smooth or rough, with them is right or wrong:

In the bright Muse though thousand charms conspire,

Her voice is all these tuneful fools admire;

(Who haunt Parnassus but to please their ear,

(Not mend their minds; as some to Church repair,

(Not for the doctrine, but the music there.

These equal syllables alone require,

Tho' oft the ear the open vowe's tire;

While expletives their feeble aid do join;

And ten low words oft creep in one dull line:

While they ring round the same unvary'd chimes,

With sure returns of still expected rhymes;

Where-e'er you find "the cooling western breeze,"

In the next line, it "whispers through the trees:"

If crystal streams "with pleasing murmurs creep,"

The reader's threaten'd (not in vain) with "sleep:"

Then, at the last and only couplet fraught

With some unmeaning thing they call a thought,

A needless Alexandrine ends the song

That, like a wounded snake, drags its slow length along.

Leave such to tune their own dull rhymes, and know

What's roundly smooth or languishingly slow;

And praise the easy vigour of a line,

Where Denham's strength, and Waller's sweetness join.

True ease in writing comes from art, not chance,

As those move easiest who have learn'd to dance.

'Tis not enough no harshness gives offence,

The sound must seem an Echo to the sense:

Soft is the strain when Zephyr gently blows,

And the smooth stream in smoother numbers flows;

But when loud surges lash the sounding shore,

The hoarse, rough verse should like the torrent roar:

When Ajax strives some rock's vast weight to throw,

The line too labours, and the words move slow;

Not so, when swift Camilla scours the plain,

Flies o'er th' unbending corn, and skims along the main.

Hear how Timotheus' varied lays surprize,

And bid alternate passions fall and rise!

While, at each change, the son of Libyan Jove

Now burns with glory, and then melts with love,

Now his fierce eyes with sparkling fury glow,

Now sighs steal out, and tears begin to flow:

Persians and Greeks like turns of nature found,

And the world's victor stood subdu'd by Sound!

The pow'r of Music all our hearts allow,

And what Timotheus was, is Dryden now.

Avoid Extremes; and shun the fault of such,

Who still are pleas'd too little or too much.

At ev'ry trifle scorn to take offence,

That always shows great pride, or little sense;

Those heads, as stomachs, are not sure the best,

Which nauseate all, and nothing can digest.

Yet let not each gay Turn thy rapture move;

For fools admire, but men of sense approve:

As things seem large which we thro' mists descry,

Dulness is ever apt to magnify.

Some foreign writers, some our own despise;

The Ancients only, or the Moderns prize.

Thus Wit, like Faith, by each man is apply'd

To one small sect, and all are damn'd beside.

Meanly they seek the blessing to confine,

And force that sun but on a part to shine,

Which not alone the southern wit sublimes,

But ripens spirits in cold northern climes;

Which from the first has shone on ages past,

Enlights the present, and shall warm the last;

Tho' each may feel increases and decays,

And see now clearer and now darker days.

Regard not then if Wit be old or new,

But blame the false, and value still the true.

Some ne'er advance a Judgment of their own,

But catch the spreading notion of the Town;

They reason and conclude by precedent,

And own stale nonsense which they ne'er invent.

Some judge of author's names, not works, and then

Nor praise nor blame the writings, but the men.

Of all this servile herd the worst is he

That in proud dulness joins with Quality,

A constant Critic at the great man's board,

To fetch and carry nonsense for my Lord.

What woful stuff this madrigal would be,

In some starv'd hackney sonneteer, or me?

But let a Lord once own the happy lines,

How the wit brightens! how the style refines!

Before his sacred name flies ev'ry fault,

And each exalted stanza teems with thought!

The Vulgar thus through Imitation err;

As oft the Learn'd by being singular;

So much they scorn the crowd, that if the throng

By chance go right, they purposely go wrong;

So Schismatics the plain believers quit,

And are but damn'd for having too much wit.

Some praise at morning what they blame at night;

But always think the last opinion right.

A Muse by these is like a mistress us'd,

This hour she's idoliz'd, the next abus'd;

While their weak heads like towns unfortify'd,

'Twixt sense and nonsense daily change their side.

Ask them the cause; they're wiser still, they say;

And still to-morrow's wiser than to-day.

We think our fathers fools, so wise we grow,

Our wiser sons, no doubt, will think us so.

Once School-divines this zealous isle o'er-spread;

Who knew most Sentences, was deepest read;

Faith, Gospel, all, seem'd made to be disputed,

And none had sense enough to be confuted:

Scotists and Thomists, now, in peace remain,

Amidst their kindred cobwebs in Duck-lane.

If Faith itself has diff'rent dresses worn,

What wonder modes in Wit should take their turn?

Oft', leaving what is natural and fit,

The current folly proves the ready wit;

And authors think their reputation safe,

Which lives as long as fools are pleas'd to laugh.

Some valuing those of their own side or mind,

Still make themselves the measure of mankind:

Fondly we think we honour merit then,

When we but praise ourselves in other men.

Parties in Wit attend on those of State,

And public faction doubles private hate.

Pride, Malice, Folly, against Dryden rose,

In various shapes of Parsons, Critics, Beaus;

But sense surviv'd, when merry jests were past;

For rising merit will buoy up at last.

Might he return, and bless once more our eyes,

New Blackmores and new Milbourns must arise:

Nay should great Homer lift his awful head,

Zoilus again would start up from the dead.

Envy will merit, as its shade, pursue;

But like a shadow, proves the substance true;

For envy'd Wit, like Sol eclips'd, makes known

Th' opposing body's grossness, not its own,

When first that sun too pow'rful beams displays,

It draws up vapours which obscure its rays;

But ev'n those clouds at last adorn its way,

Reflect new glories, and augment the day.

Be thou the first true merit to befriend;

His praise is lost, who stays, till all commend.

Short is the date, alas, of modern rhymes,

And 'tis but just to let them live betimes.

No longer now that golden age appears,

When Patriarch-wits surviv'd a thousand years:

Now length of Fame (our second life) is lost,

And bare threescore is all ev'n that can boast;

Our sons their fathers' failing language see,

And such as Chaucer is, shall Dryden be.

So when the faithful pencil has design'd

Some bright Idea of the master's mind,

Where a new world leaps out at his command,

And ready Nature waits upon his hand;

When the ripe colours soften and unite,

And sweetly melt into just shade and light;

When mellowing years their full perfection give,

And each bold figure just begins to live,

The treach'rous colours the fair art betray,

And all the bright creation fades away!

Unhappy Wit, like most mistaken things,

Atones not for that envy which it brings.

In youth alone its empty praise we boast,

But soon the short-liv'd vanity is lost:

Like some fair flow'r the early spring supplies.

That gaily blooms, but ev'n in blooming dies.

What is this Wit, which must our cares employ?

The owner's wife, that other men enjoy;

Then most our trouble still when most admir'd,

And still the more we give, the more requir'd;

Whose fame with pains we guard, but lose with ease,

Sure some to vex, but never all to please;

'Tis what the vicious fear, the virtuous shun,

By fools't is hated, and by knaves undone!

If Wit so much from Ign'rance undergo,

Ah let not Learning too commence its foe!

Of old, those met rewards who could excel,

And such were prais'd who but endeavour'd well:

Tho' triumphs were to gen'rals only due,

Crowns were reserv'd to grace the soldiers too,

Now, they who reach Parnassus' lofty crown,

Employ their pains to spurn some others down;

And while self-love each jealous writer rules,

Contending wits become the sport of fools:

But still the worst with most regret commend,

For each ill Author is as bad a Friend.

To what base ends, and by what abject ways,

Are mortals urg'd thro' sacred lust of praise!

Ah ne'er so dire a thirst of glory boast,

Nor in the Critic let the Man be lost.

Good-nature and good-sense must ever join;

To err is human, to forgive, divine.

But if in noble minds some dregs remain

Not yet purg'd off, of spleen and sour disdain;

Discharge that rage on more provoking crimes,

Nor fear a dearth in these flagitious times.

No pardon vile Obscenity should find,

Tho' wit and art conspire to move your mind;

But Dulness with Obscenity must prove

As shameful sure as Impotence in love.

In the fat age of pleasure wealth and ease

Sprung the rank weed, and thriv'd with large increase:

When love was all an easy Monarch's care;

Seldom at council, never in a war:

Jilts rul'd the state, and statesmen farces writ;

Nay wits had pensions, and young Lords had wit:

The Fair sate panting at a Courtier's play,

And not a Mask went unimprov'd away:

The modest fan was lifted up no more,

And Virgins smil'd at what they blush'd before.

The following licence of a Foreign reign

Did all the dregs of bold Socinus drain;

Then unbelieving priests reform'd the nation,

And taught more pleasant methods of salvation;

Where Heav'n's free subjects might their rights dispute,

Lest God himself should seem too absolute:

Pulpits their sacred satire learn'd to spare,

And Vice admir'd to find a flatt'rer there!

Encourag'd thus, Wit's Titans brav'd the skies,

And the press groan'd with licens'd blasphemies.

These monsters, Critics! with your darts engage,

Here point your thunder, and exhaust your rage!

Yet shun their fault, who, scandalously nice,

Will needs mistake an author into vice;

All seems infected that th' infected spy,

As all looks yellow to the jaundic'd eye.

Learn then what Morals Critics ought to show,

For't is but half a Judge's task, to know.

'Tis not enough, taste, judgment, learning, join;

In all you speak, let truth and candour shine:

That not alone what to your sense is due

All may allow; but seek your friendship too.

Be silent always when you doubt your sense;

And speak, tho' sure, with seeming diffidence:

Some positive, persisting fops we know,

Who, if once wrong, will needs be always so;

But you, with pleasure own your errors past,

And make each day a Critic on the last.

'T is not enough, your counsel still be true;

Blunt truths more mischief than nice falsehoods do;

Men must be taught as if you taught them not,

And things unknown propos'd as things forgot.

Without Good Breeding, truth is disapprov'd;

That only makes superior sense belov'd.

Be niggards of advice on no pretence;

For the worst avarice is that of sense.

With mean complacence ne'er betray your trust,

Nor be so civil as to prove unjust.

Fear not the anger of the wise to raise;

Those best can bear reproof, who merit praise.

'T were well might critics still this freedom take,

But Appius reddens at each word you speak,

And stares, tremendous, with a threat'ning eye,

Like some fierce Tyrant in old tapestry.

Fear most to tax an Honourable fool,

Whose right it is, uncensur'd, to be dull;

Such, without wit, are Poets when they please,

As without learning they can take Degrees.

Leave dang'rous truths to unsuccessful Satires,

And flattery to fulsome Dedicators,

Whom, when they praise, the world believes no more,

Than when they promise to give scribbling o'er.

'T is best sometimes your censure to restrain,

And charitably let the dull be vain:

Your silence there is better than your spite,

For who can rail so long as they can write?

Still humming on, their drowsy course they keep,

And lash'd so long, like tops, are lash'd asleep.

False steps but help them to renew the race,

As, after stumbling, Jades will mend their pace.

What crowds of these, impenitently bold,

In sounds and jingling syllables grown old,

Still run on Poets, in a raging vein,

Ev'n to the dregs and squeezings of the brain,

Strain out the last dull droppings of their sense,

And rhyme with all the rage of Impotence.

Such shameless Bards we have; and yet't is true,

There are as mad abandon'd Critics too.

The bookful blockhead, ignorantly read,

With loads of learned lumber in his head,

With his own tongue still edifies his ears,

And always list'ning to himself appears.

All books he reads, and all he reads assails.

From Dryden's Fables down to Durfey's Tales.

With him, most authors steal their works, or buy;

Garth did not write his own Dispensary.

Name a new Play, and he's the Poet's friend,

Nay show'd his faults — but when would Poets mend?

No place so sacred from such fops is barr'd,

Nor is Paul's church more safe than Paul's churchyard:

Nay, fly to Altars; there they'll talk you dead:

For Fools rush in where Angels fear to tread.

(Distrustful sense with modest caution speaks,

(It still looks home, and short excursions makes;

(But rattling nonsense in full volleys breaks,

And never shock'd, and never turn'd aside,

Bursts out, resistless, with a thund'ring tide.

But where's the man, who counsel can bestow,

Still pleas'd to teach, and yet not proud to know?

Unbiass'd, or by favour, or by spite;

Not dully prepossess'd, nor blindly right;

Tho' learn'd, well-bred; and tho' well-bred, sincere,

Modestly bold, and humanly severe:

Who to a friend his faults can freely show,

And gladly praise the merit of a foe?

Blest with a taste exact, yet unconfin'd;

A knowledge both of books and human kind:

Gen'rous converse; a soul exempt from pride;

And love to praise, with reason on his side?

Such once were Critics; such the happy few,

Athens and Rome in better ages knew.

The mighty Stagirite first left the shore,

Spread all his sails, and durst the deeps explore:

He steer'd securely, and discover'd far,

Led by the light of the Mæonian Star.

Poets, a race long unconfin'd, and free,

Still fond and proud of savage liberty,

Receiv'd his laws; and stood convinc'd 't was fit,

Who conquer'd Nature, should preside o'er Wit.

Horace still charms with graceful negligence,

And without method talks us into sense,

Will, like a friend, familiarly convey

The truest notions in the easiest way.

He, who supreme in judgment, as in wit,

Might boldly censure, as he boldly writ,

Yet judg'd with coolness, tho' he sung with fire;

His Precepts teach but what his works inspire.

Our Critics take a contrary extreme,

They judge with fury, but they write with fle'me:

Nor suffers Horace more in wrong Translations

By Wits, than Critics in as wrong Quotations.

See Dionysius Homer's thoughts refine,

And call new beauties forth from ev'ry line!

Fancy and art in gay Petronius please,

The scholar's learning, with the courtier's ease.

In grave Quintilian's copious work, we find

The justest rules, and clearest method join'd:

Thus useful arms in magazines we place,

All rang'd in order, and dispos'd with grace,

But less to please the eye, than arm the hand,

Still fit for use, and ready at command.

Thee, bold Longinus! all the Nine inspire,

And bless their Critic with a Poet's fire.

An ardent Judge, who zealous in his trust,

With warmth gives sentence, yet is always just;

Whose own example strengthens all his laws;

And is himself that great Sublime he draws.

Thus long succeeding Critics justly reign'd,

Licence repress'd, and useful laws ordain'd.

Learning and Rome alike in empire grew;

And Arts still follow'd where her Eagles flew;

From the same foes, at last, both felt their doom,

And the same age saw Learning fall, and Rome.

With Tyranny, then Superstition join'd,

As that the body, this enslav'd the mind;

Much was believ'd, but little understood,

And to be dull was constru'd to be good;

A second deluge Learning thus o'er-run,

And the Monks finish'd what the Goths begun.

At length Erasmus, that great injur'd name,

(The glory of the Priesthood, and the shame!)

Stemm'd the wild torrent of a barb'rous age,

And drove those holy Vandals off the stage.

But see! each Muse, in Leo's golden days,

Starts from her trance, and trims her wither'd bays,

Rome's ancient Genius, o'er its ruins spread,

Shakes off the dust, and rears his rev'rend head.

Then Sculpture and her sister-arts revive;

Stones leap'd to form, and rocks began to live;

With sweeter notes each rising Temple rung;

A Raphael painted, and a Vida sung.

Immortal Vida: on whose honour'd brow

The Poet's bays and Critic's ivy grow:

Cremona now shal ever boast thy name,

As next in place to Mantua, next in fame!

But soon by impious arms from Latium chas'd,

Their ancient bounds the banish'd Muses pass'd;

Thence Arts o'er all the northern world advance,

But Critic-learning flourish'd most in France:

The rules a nation, born to serve, obeys;

And Boileau still in right of Horace sways.

But we, brave Britons, foreign laws despis'd,

And kept unconquer'd, and unciviliz'd;

Fierce for the liberties of wit, and bold,

We still defy'd the Romans, as of old.

Yet some there were, among the sounder few

Of those who less presum'd, and better knew,

Who durst assert the juster ancient cause,

And here restor'd Wit's fundamental laws.

Such was the Muse, whose rules and practice tell,

"Nature's chief Master-piece is writing well."

Such was Roscommon, not more learn'd than good,

With manners gen'rous as his noble blood;

To him the wit of Greece and Rome was known,

And ev'ry author's merit, but his own.

Such late was Walsh — the Muse's judge and friend,

Who justly knew to blame or to commend;

To failings mild, but zealous for desert;

The clearest head, and the sincerest heart.

This humble praise, lamented shade! receive,

This praise at least a grateful Muse may give:

The Muse, whose early voice you taught to sing,

Prescrib'd her heights, and prun'd her tender wing,

(Her guide now lost) no more attempts to rise,

But in low numbers short excursions tries:

Content, if hence th' unlearn'd their wants may view,

The learn'd reflect on what before they knew:

Careless of censure, nor too fond of fame;

Still pleas'd to praise, yet not afraid to blame,

Averse alike to flatter, or offend;

Not free from faults, nor yet too vain to mend.

5

10

15

20

25

30

35

40

45

50

55

60

65

70

75

80

85

90

95

100

105

110

115

120

125

130

135

140

145

150

155

160

165

170

175

180

185

190

195

200

205

210

215

220

225

230

235

240

245

250

255

260

265

270

275

280

285

290

295

300

305

310

315

320

325

330

335

340

345

350

355

360

365

370

375

380

385

390

395

400

405

410

415

420

425

430

435

440

445

450

455

460

465

470

475

480

485

490

495

500

505

510

515

520

525

530

535

540

545

550

555

560

565

570

575

580

585

590

595

600

605

610

615

620

625

630

635

640

645

650

655

660

665

670

675

680

685

690

695

700

705

710

715

720

725

730

735

740

Contents

Having proposed to write some pieces on Human Life and
Manners, such as (to use my Lord Bacon's expression) come home
to Men's Business and Bosoms, I thought it more satisfactory to
begin with considering Man in the abstract, his Nature and his
State; since, to prove any moral duty, to enforce any moral precept,
or to examine the perfection or imperfection of any creature
whatsoever, it is necessary first to know what condition and
relation it is placed in, and what is the proper end and purpose of
its being.

The science of Human Nature is, like all other sciences, reduced to
a few clear points: There are not many certain truths in this world.
It is therefore in the Anatomy of the mind as in that of the Body;
more good will accrue to mankind by attending to the large, open,
and perceptible parts, than by studying too much such finer nerves
and vessels, the conformations and uses of which will for ever

escape our observation. The disputes are all upon these last, and, I will venture to say, they have less sharpened the wits than the hearts of men against each other, and have diminished the practice, more than advanced the theory of Morality. If I could flatter myself that this Essay has any merit, it is in steering betwixt the extremes of doctrines seemingly opposite, in passing over terms utterly unintelligible, and in forming a temperate yet not inconsistent, and a short yet not imperfect system of Ethics.

This I might have done in prose, but I chose verse, and even rhyme, for two reasons. The one will appear obvious; that principles, maxims, or precepts so written, both strike the reader more strongly at first, and are more easily retained by him afterwards: The other may seem odd, but is true, I found I could express them more shortly this way than in prose itself; and nothing is more certain, than that much of the force as well as grace of arguments or instructions, depends on their conciseness. I was unable to treat this part of my subject more in detail, without becoming dry and tedious; or more poetically, without sacrificing perspicuity to ornament, without wandring from the precision, or breaking the chain of reasoning: If any man can unite all these without diminution of any of them, I freely confess he will compass a thing above my capacity.

What is now published, is only to be considered as a general Map of Man, marking out no more than the greater parts, their extent, their limits, and their connection, and leaving the particular to be more fully delineated in the charts which are to follow. Consequently, these Epistles in their progress (if I have health and leisure to make any progress) will be less dry, and more susceptible of poetical ornament. I am here only opening the fountains, and clearing the passage. To deduce the rivers, to follow them in their course, and to observe their effects, may be a task more agreeable.

P.

Contents

Argument of Epistle I

Of the Nature and State of Man, with respect to the Universe.

Of Man in the abstract.

That we can judge only with regard to our own system, being ignorant of the relations of systems and things.

II   35 &c.

That

Man is not to be deemed imperfect, but a Being suited to his place and rank in the creation, agreeable to the general Order of things, and conformable to Ends and Relations to him unknown.

III   77 &c.

That it

is partly upon his ignorance of future events, and partly upon the hope of a future state, that all his happiness in the present depends.

IV   109 &c.

The

pride of aiming at more knowledge, and pretending to more Perfections, the cause of Man's error and misery. The impiety of putting himself in the place of God, and judging of the fitness or unfitness, perfection or imperfection, justice or injustice of his dispensations.

V   131 &c.

The

absurdity of conceiting himself the final cause of the creation, or expecting that perfection in the moral world, which is not in the natural.

VI   173 &c.

The

unreasonableness of his complaints against Providence, while on the one hand he demands the Perfections of the Angels, and on the other the bodily qualifications of the Brutes; though, to possess any of the sensitive faculties in a higher degree, would render him miserable.

VII   207

That

throughout the whole visible world, an universal order and gradation in the sensual and mental faculties is observed, which causes a subordination of creature to creature, and of all creatures to Man. The gradations of sense, instinct, thought, reflection, reason; that Reason alone countervails fill the other faculties.

VIII   233
                                                       How
much further this order and subordination of living creatures may extend, above and below us; were any part of which broken, not that part only, but the whole connected creation must be destroyed.

IX   250 The
extravagance, madness, and pride of such a desire.

X

                                                  281 →e
nd   The
consequence of all, the absolute submission due to Providence, both as to our present and future state.

Contents

Epistle I

                                                   Awake,
my St. John! leave all meaner things

To low ambition, and the pride of Kings.

Let us (since Life can little more supply

Than just to look about us and to die)

Expatiate free o'er all this scene of Man;

A mighty maze! but not without a plan;

A Wild, where weeds and flow'rs promiscuous shoot;

Or Garden, tempting with forbidden fruit.

Together let us beat this ample field,

Try what the open, what the covert yield;

The latent tracts, the giddy heights, explore

Of all who blindly creep, or sightless soar;

Eye Nature's walks, shoot Folly as it flies,

And catch the Manners living as they rise;

Laugh where we must, be candid where we can;

But vindicate the ways of God to Man.

5

10

15

I   Say
first, of God above, or Man below,

What can we reason, but from what we know?

Of Man, what see we but his station here,

From which to reason, or to which refer?

Thro' worlds unnumber'd tho' the God be known,

'Tis ours to trace him only in our own.

He, who thro' vast immensity can pierce,

See worlds on worlds compose one universe,

Observe how system into system runs,

What other planets circle other suns,

What vary'd Being peoples ev'ry star,

May tell why Heav'n has made us as we are.

But of this frame the bearings, and the ties,

The strong connexions, nice dependencies,

Gradations just, has thy pervading soul

Look'd thro'? or can a part contain the whole?

Is the great chain, that draws all to agree,

And drawn supports, upheld by God, or thee?

20

25

30

II

Presum

ptuous Man! the reason wouldst thou find,

Why form'd so weak, so little, and so blind?

First, if thou canst, the harder reason guess,

Why form'd no weaker, blinder, and no less?

Ask of thy mother earth, why oaks are made

Taller or stronger than the weeds they shade?

Or ask of yonder argent fields above,

Why Jove's satellites are less than Jove?

Of Systems possible, if 'tis confest

That Wisdom infinite must form the best,

Where all must full or not coherent be,

And all that rises, rise in due degree;

Then, in the scale of reas'ning life, 'tis plain,

There must be, somewhere, such a rank as Man:

And all the question (wrangle e'er so long)

Is only this, if God has plac'd him wrong?

Respecting Man, whatever wrong we call,

May, must be right, as relative to all.

In human works, tho' labour'd on with pain,

A thousand movements scarce one purpose gain;

In God's, one single can its end produce;

Yet serves to second too some other use.

So Man, who here seems principal alone,

Perhaps acts second to some sphere unknown,

Touches some wheel, or verges to some goal;

'Tis but a part we see, and not a whole.

When the proud steed shall know why Man restrains

His fiery course, or drives him o'er the plains:

When the dull Ox, why now he breaks the clod,

Is now a victim, and now Ægypt's God:

Then shall Man's pride and dulness comprehend

His actions', passions', being's, use and end;

Why doing, suff'ring, check'd, impell'd; and why

This hour a slave, the next a deity.

Then say not Man's imperfect, Heav'n in fault;

Say rather, Man's as perfect as he ought:

His knowledge measur'd to his state and place;

His time a moment, and a point his space.

If to be perfect in a certain sphere,

What matter, soon or late, or here or there?

The blest to day is as completely so,,

As who began a thousand years ago.   35

40

45

50

55

60

65

70

75

III   Heav'n
from all creatures hides the book of Fate,

All but the page prescrib'd, their present state:

From brutes what men, from men what spirits know:

Or who could suffer Being here below?

The lamb thy riot dooms to bleed to-day,

Had he thy Reason, would he skip and play?

Pleas'd to the last, he crops the flow'ry food,

And licks the hand just rais'd to shed his blood.

Oh blindness to the future! kindly giv'n,

That each may fill the circle mark'd by Heav'n:

Who sees with equal eye, as God of all,

A hero perish, or a sparrow fall,

Atoms or systems into ruin hurl'd,

And now a bubble burst, and now a world.

Hope humbly then: with trembling pinions soar;

Wait the great teacher Death; and God adore.

What future bliss, he gives not thee to know,

But gives that Hope to be thy blessing now.

Hope springs eternal in the human breast:

Man never Is, but always To be blest:

The soul, uneasy and confin'd from home,

Rests and expatiates in a life to come.

Lo, the poor Indian! whose untutor'd mind

Sees God in clouds, or hears him in the wind:

His soul, proud Science never taught to stray

Far as the solar walk, or milky way;

Yet simple Nature to his hope has giv'n,

Behind the cloud-topt hill, an humbler heav'n;

Some safer world in depth of woods embrac'd,

Some happier island in the watry waste,

Where slaves once more their native land behold,

No fiends torment, no Christians thirst for gold.

To Be, contents his natural desire,

He asks no Angel's wing, no Seraph's fire;

But thinks, admitted to that equal sky,

His faithful dog shall bear him company.

80

85

90

95

100

105

110

IV   Go,
wiser thou! and, in thy scale of sense,

Weight thy Opinion against Providence;

Call imperfection what thou fancy'st such,

Say, here he gives too little, there too much:

Destroy all Creatures for thy sport or gust,

Yet cry, If Man's unhappy, God's unjust;

If Man alone engross not Heav'n's high care,

Alone made perfect here, immortal there:

Snatch from his hand the balance and the rod,

Re-judge his justice, be the God of God.

In Pride, in reas'ning Pride, our error lies;

All quit their sphere, and rush into the skies.

Pride still is aiming at the blest abodes,

Men would be Angels, Angels would be Gods.

Aspiring to be Gods, if Angels fell,

Aspiring to be Angels, Men rebel:

And who but wishes to invert the laws

Of Order, sins against th' Eternal Cause.

115

120

125

130

V   Ask for

what end the heav'nly bodies shine,

Earth for whose use? Pride answers, "'Tis for mine:

For me kind Nature wakes her genial Pow'r,

Suckles each herb, and spreads out ev'ry flow'r;

Annual for me, the grape, the rose renew

The juice nectareous, and the balmy dew;

For me, the mine a thousand treasures brings;

For me, health gushes from a thousand springs;

Seas roll to waft me, suns to light me rise;

My foot-stool earth, my canopy the skies."

But errs not Nature from his gracious end,

From burning suns when livid deaths descend,

When earthquakes swallow, or when tempests sweep

Towns to one grave, whole nations to the deep?

"No, ('tis reply'd) the first Almighty Cause

Acts not by partial, but by gen'ral laws;

Th' exceptions few; some change since all began:

And what created perfect?" — Why then Man?

If the great end be human Happiness,

Then Nature deviates; and can Man do less?

As much that end a constant course requires

Of show'rs and sun-shine, as of Man's desires;

As much eternal springs and cloudless skies,

As Men for ever temp'rate, calm, and wise.

If plagues or earthquakes break not Heav'n's design,

Why then a Borgia, or a Catiline?

Who knows but he, whose hand the lightning forms,

Who heaves old Ocean, and who wings the storms;

Pours fierce Ambition in a Caesar's mind,

Or turns young Ammon loose to scourge mankind?

From pride, from pride, our very reas'ning springs;

Account for moral, as for nat'ral things:

Why charge we Heav'n in those, in these acquit?

In both, to reason right is to submit.

Better for Us, perhaps, it might appear,

Were there all harmony, all virtue here;

That never air or ocean felt the wind;

That never passion discompos'd the mind.

But All subsists by elemental strife;

And Passions are the elements of Life.

The gen'ral Order, since the whole began,

Is kept in Nature, and is kept in Man.

135

140

145

150

155

160

165

170

VI   What
would this Man? Now upward will he soar,

And little less than Angel, would be more;

Now looking downwards, just as griev'd appears

To want the strength of bulls, the fur of bears.

Made for his use all creatures if he call,

Say what their use, had he the pow'rs of all?

Nature to these, without profusion, kind,

The proper organs, proper pow'rs assign'd;

Each seeming want compensated of course,

Here with degrees of swiftness, there of force;

All in exact proportion to the state;

Nothing to add, and nothing to abate.

Each beast, each insect, happy in its own:

Is Heav'n unkind to Man, and Man alone?

Shall he alone, whom rational we call,

Be pleas'd with nothing, if not bless'd with all?

The bliss of Man (could Pride that blessing find)

Is not to act or think beyond mankind;

No pow'rs of body or of soul to share,

But what his nature and his state can bear.

Why has not Man a microscopic eye?

For this plain reason, Man is not a Fly.

Say what the use, were finer optics giv'n,

T' inspect a mite, not comprehend the heav'n?

Or touch, if tremblingly alive all o'er,

To smart and agonize at every pore?

Or quick effluvia darting thro' the brain,

Die of a rose in aromatic pain?

If Nature thunder'd in his op'ning ears,

And stunn'd him with the music of the spheres,

How would he wish that Heav'n had left him still

The whisp'ring Zephyr, and the purling rill?

Who finds not Providence all good and wise,

Alike in what it gives, and what denies?

175

180

185

190

195

200

205

VII   Far as
Creation's ample range extends,

The scale of sensual, mental pow'rs ascends:

Mark how it mounts, to Man's imperial race,

From the green myriads in the peopled grass:

What modes of sight betwixt each wide extreme,

The mole's dim curtain, and the lynx's beam:

Of smell, the headlong lioness between,

And hound sagacious on the tainted green:

Of hearing, from the life that fills the Flood,

To that which warbles thro' the vernal wood:

The spider's touch, how exquisitely fine!

Feels at each thread, and lives along the line:

In the nice bee, what sense so subtly true

From pois'nous herbs extracts the healing dew?

How Instinct varies in the grov'lling swine,

Compar'd, half-reas'ning elephant, with thine!

'Twixt that, and Reason, what a nice barrier,

For ever sep'rate, yet for ever near!

Remembrance and Reflection how ally'd;

What thin partitions Sense from Thought divide:

And Middle natures, how they long to join,

Yet never pass th' insuperable line!

Without this just gradation, could they be

Subjected, these to those, or all to thee?

The pow'rs of all subdu'd by thee alone,

Is not thy Reason all these pow'rs in one?

210

215

220

225

230

VIII   See,
thro' this air, this ocean, and this earth,

All matter quick, and bursting into birth.

Above, how high, progressive life may go!

Around, how wide! how deep extend below!

Vast chain of Being! which from God began,

Natures ethereal, human, angel, man,

Beast, bird, fish, insect, what no eye can see,

No glass can reach; from Infinite to thee,

From thee to Nothing. — On superior pow'rs

Were we to press, inferior might on ours:

Or in the full creation leave a void,

Where, one step broken, the great scale's destroy'd:

From Nature's chain whatever link you strike,

Tenth or ten thousandth, breaks the chain alike.

And, if each system in gradation roll

Alike essential to th' amazing Whole,

The least confusion but in one, not all

That system only, but the Whole must fall.

Let Earth unbalanc'd from her orbit fly,

Planets and Suns run lawless thro' the sky;

Let ruling Angels from their spheres be hurl'd,

Being on Being wreck'd, and world on world;

Heav'n's whole foundations to their centre nod,

And Nature tremble to the throne of God.

All this dread Order break — for whom? for thee?

Vile worm! — Oh Madness! Pride! Impiety!

235

240

245

250

255

IX   What if
the foot, ordain'd the dust to tread,

Or hand, to toil, aspir'd to be the head?

What if the head, the eye, or ear repin'd

To serve mere engines to the ruling Mind?

Just as absurd for any part to claim

To be another, in this gen'ral frame:

Just as absurd, to mourn the tasks or pains,

The great directing Mind of All ordains.

All are but parts of one stupendous whole,

Whose body Nature is, and God the soul;

That, chang'd thro' all, and yet in all the same;

Great in the earth, as in th' ethereal frame;

Warms in the sun, refreshes in the breeze,

Glows in the stars, and blossoms in the trees,

Lives thro' all life, extends thro' all extent,

Spreads undivided, operates unspent;

Breathes in our soul, informs our mortal part,

As full, as perfect, in a hair as heart:

As full, as perfect, in vile Man that mourns,

As the rapt Seraph that adores and burns:

To him no high, no low, no great, no small;

He fills, he bounds, connects, and equals all.

260

265

270

275

280

X   Cease
then, nor Order Imperfection name:

Our proper bliss depends on what we blame.

Know thy own point: This kind, this due degree

Of blindness, weakness, Heav'n bestows on thee.

Submit. — In this, or any other sphere,

Secure to be as blest as thou canst bear:

Safe in the hand of one disposing Pow'r,

Or in the natal, or the mortal hour.

All Nature is but Art, unknown to thee;

All Chance, Direction, which thou canst not see;

All Discord, Harmony not understood;

All partial Evil, universal Good:

And, spite of Pride, in erring Reason's spite,

One truth is clear, Whatever Is, Is Right.

285

290

Contents

Epistle to Dr. Arbuthnot

Advertisement to the first publication of this Epistle

This paper is a sort of bill of complaint, begun many years since, and drawn up by snatches, as the several occasions offered. I had no thoughts of publishing it, till it pleased some Persons of Rank and Fortune (the Authors of Verses to the Imitator of Horace, and of an Epistle to a Doctor of Divinity from a Nobleman at Hampton Court) to attack, in a very extraordinary manner, not only my Writings (of which, being public, the Public is judge), but my Person, Morals, and Family, whereof, to those who know me not, a truer information may be requisite. Being divided between the necessity to say something of myself, and my own laziness to undertake so awkward a task, I thought it the shortest way to put the last hand to this Epistle. If it have any thing pleasing, it will be that by which I am most desirous to please, the Truth and the Sentiment; and if any thing offensive, it will be only to those I am least sorry to offend, the vicious or the ungenerous.

Many will know their own pictures in it, there being not a circumstance but what is true; but I have, for the most part, spared their Names, and they may escape being laughed at, if they please.

I would have some of them know, it was owing to the request of the learned and candid Friend to whom it is inscribed, that I make not as free use of theirs as they have done of mine. However, I shall have this advantage, and honour, on my side, that whereas, by their proceeding, any abuse may be directed at any man, no injury can possibly be done by mine, since a nameless character can never be found out, but by its truth and likeness.

P.

Contents

Epistle to Dr Arnuthnot

P. shut, shut the door, good John! fatigu'd, I said,

Tie up the knocker, say I'm sick, I'm dead.

The Dog-star rages! nay't is past a doubt,

All Bedlam, or Parnassus, is let out:

Fire in each eye, and papers in each hand,

They rave, recite, and madden round the land.

What walls can guard me, or what shade can hide?

They pierce my thickets, thro' my Grot they glide;

By land, by water, they renew the charge;

They stop the chariot, and they board the barge.

No place is sacred, not the Church is free;

Ev'n Sunday shines no Sabbath-day to me;

Then from the Mint walks forth the Man of rhyme,

Happy to catch me just at Dinner-time.

Is there a Parson, much bemus'd in beer,

A maudlin Poetess, a rhyming Peer,

A Clerk, foredoom'd his father's soul to cross,

Who pens a Stanza, when he should engross?

Is there, who, lock'd from ink and paper, scrawls

With desp'rate charcoal round his darken'd walls?

All fly to Twit'nam, and in humble strain

Apply to me, to keep them mad or vain.

Arthur, whose giddy son neglects the Laws,

Imputes to me and my damn'd works the cause:

Poor Cornus sees his frantic wife elope,

And curses Wit, and Poetry, and Pope.

Friend to my Life! (which did not you prolong,

The world had wanted many an idle song)

What Drop or Nostrum can this plague remove?

Or which must end me, a Fool's wrath or love?

A dire dilemma! either way I'm sped,

If foes, they write, if friends, they read me dead.

Seiz'd and tied down to judge, how wretched I!

Who can't be silent, and who will not lie.

To laugh, were want of goodness and of grace,

And to be grave, exceeds all Pow'r of face.

I sit with sad civility, I read

With honest anguish, and an aching head;

And drop at last, but in unwilling ears,

This saving counsel, "Keep your piece nine years."

"Nine years!" cries he, who high in Drury-lane,

Lull'd by soft Zephyrs thro' the broken pane,

Rhymes ere he wakes, and prints before Term ends,

Oblig'd by hunger, and request of friends:

"The piece, you think, is incorrect? why, take it,

I'm all submission, what you'd have it, make it."

Three things another's modest wishes bound,

My Friendship, and a Prologue, and ten pound.

Pitholeon sends to me: "You know his Grace

I want a Patron; ask him for a Place."

"Pitholeon libell'd me," — "but here's a letter

Informs you, Sir, 't was when he knew no better.

Dare you refuse him? Curll invites to dine",

"He'll write a Journal, or he'll turn Divine."

Bless me! a packet. — "'Tis a stranger sues,

A Virgin Tragedy, an Orphan Muse."

If I dislike it, "Furies, death and rage!"

If I approve, "Commend it to the Stage."

There (thank my stars) my whole Commission ends,

The Play'rs and I are, luckily, no friends,

Fir'd that the house reject him, "'Sdeath I'll print it,

And shame the fools — Your Int'rest, Sir, with Lintot!"

'Lintot, dull rogue! will think your price too much:'

"Not, Sir, if you revise it, and retouch."

All my demurs but double his Attacks;

At last he whispers, "Do; and we go snacks."

Glad of a quarrel, straight I clap the door,

Sir, let me see your works and you no more.

'Tis sung, when Midas' Ears began to spring,

(Midas, a sacred person and a king)

His very Minister who spy'd them first,

(Some say his Queen) was forc'd to speak, or burst.

And is not mine, my friend, a sorer case,

When ev'ry coxcomb perks them in my face?

A. Good friend, forbear! you deal in dang'rous things.

I'd never name Queens, Ministers, or Kings;

Keep close to Ears, and those let asses prick;

'Tis nothing — P. Nothing? if they bite and kick?

Out with it, Dunciad! let the secret pass,

That secret to each fool, that he's an Ass:

The truth once told (and wherefore should we lie?)

The Queen of Midas slept, and so may I.

You think this cruel? take it for a rule,

No creature smarts so little as a fool.

Let peals of laughter, Codrus! round thee break,

Thou unconcern'd canst hear the mighty crack:

Pit, Box, and gall'ry in convulsions hurl'd,

Thou stand'st unshook amidst a bursting world.

Who shames a Scribbler? break one cobweb thro',

He spins the slight, self-pleasing thread anew:

Destroy his fib or sophistry, in vain,

The creature's at his dirty work again,

Thron'd in the centre of his thin designs,

Proud of a vast extent of flimsy lines!

Whom have I hurt? has Poet yet, or Peer

Lost the arch'd eye-brow, or Parnassian sneer?

* * * * *

Does not one table Bavius still admit?

Still to one Bishop Philips seem a wit?

Still Sappho — A. Hold! for God's sake — you 'll offend,

No Names! — be calm! — learn prudence of a friend!

I too could write, and I am twice as tall;

But foes like these — P. One Flatt'rer's worse than all.

Of all mad creatures, if the learn'd are right,

It is the slaver kills, and not the bite.

A fool quite angry is quite innocent:

Alas! 'tis ten times worse when they repent.

One dedicates in high heroic prose,

And ridicules beyond a hundred foes:

One from all Grubstreet will my fame defend,

And more abusive, calls himself my friend.

This prints my Letters, that expects a bribe,

And others roar aloud, "Subscribe, subscribe."

There are, who to my person pay their court:

I cough like Horace, and, tho' lean, am short,

Ammon's great son one shoulder had too high,

Such Ovid's nose, and "Sir! you have an Eye" —

Go on, obliging creatures, make me see

All that disgrac'd my Betters, met in me.

Say for my comfort, languishing in bed,

"Just so immortal Maro held his head:"

And when I die, be sure you let me know

Great Homer died three thousand years ago.

Why did I write? what sin to me unknown

Dipt me in ink, my parents', or my own?

As yet a child, nor yet a fool to fame,

I lisp'd in numbers, for the numbers came.

I left no calling for this idle trade,

No duty broke, no father disobey'd.

The Muse but serv'd to ease some friend, not Wife,

To help me thro' this long disease, my Life,

To second, Arbuthnot! thy Art and Care,

And teach the Being you preserv'd, to bear.

But why then publish? Granville the polite,

And knowing Walsh, would tell me I could write;

Well-natur'd Garth inflam'd with early praise;

And Congreve lov'd, and Swift endur'd my lays;

The courtly Talbot, Somers, Sheffield, read;

Ev'n mitred Rochester would nod the head,

And St. John's self (great Dryden's friends before)

With open arms receiv'd one Poet more.

Happy my studies, when by these approv'd!

Happier their author, when by these belov'd!

From these the world will judge of men and books,

Not from the Burnets, Oldmixons, and Cookes.

Soft were my numbers; who could take offence,

While pure Description held the place of Sense?

Like gentle Fanny's was my flow'ry theme,

A painted mistress, or a purling stream.

Yet then did Gildon draw his venal quill; —

I wish'd the man a dinner, and sat still.

Yet then did Dennis rave in furious fret;

I never answer'd, — I was not in debt.

If want provok'd, or madness made them print,

I wag'd no war with Bedlam or the Mint.

Did some more sober Critic come abroad;

If wrong, I smil'd; if right, I kiss'd the rod.

Pains, reading, study, are their just pretence,

And all they want is spirit, taste, and sense.

Commas and points they set exactly right,

And 'twere a sin to rob them of their mite.

Yet ne'er one sprig of laurel grac'd these ribalds,

From slashing Bentley down to pidling Tibalds:

Each wight, who reads not, and but scans and spells,

Each Word-catcher, that lives on syllables,

Ev'n such small Critics some regard may claim,

Preserv'd in Milton's or in Shakespeare's name.

Pretty! in amber to observe the forms

Of hairs, or straws, or dirt, or grubs, or worms!

The things, we know, are neither rich nor rare,

But wonder how the devil they got there.

Were others angry: I excus'd them too;

Well might they rage, I gave them but their due.

A man's true merit 'tis not hard to find;

But each man's secret standard in his mind,

That Casting-weight pride adds to emptiness,

This, who can gratify? for who can guess?

The Bard whom pilfer'd Pastorals renown,

Who turns a Persian tale for half a Crown,

Just writes to make his barrenness appear,

And strains, from hard-bound brains, eight lines a year;

He, who still wanting, tho' he lives on theft,

Steals much, spends little, yet has nothing left:

And He, who now to sense, now nonsense leaning,

Means not, but blunders round about a meaning:

And He, whose fustian's so sublimely bad,

It is not Poetry, but prose run mad:

All these, my modest Satire bade translate,

And own'd that nine such Poets made a Tate.

How did they fume, and stamp, and roar, and chafe!

And swear, not Addison himself was safe.

Peace to all such! but were there One whose fires

True Genius kindles, and fair Fame inspires;

Blest with each talent and each art to please,

And born to write, converse, and live with ease:

Should such a man, too fond to rule alone,

Bear, like the Turk, no brother near the throne.

View him with scornful, yet with jealous eyes,

And hate for arts that caus'd himself to rise;

Damn with faint praise, assent with civil leer,

And without sneering, teach the rest to sneer;

Willing to wound, and yet afraid to strike,

Just hint a fault, and hesitate dislike;

Alike reserv'd to blame, or to commend.

A tim'rous foe, and a suspicious friend;

Dreading ev'n fools, by Flatterers besieg'd,

And so obliging, that he ne'er oblig'd;

Like Cato, give his little Senate laws,

And sit attentive to his own applause;

While Wits and Templars ev'ry sentence raise,

And wonder with a foolish face of praise: —

Who but must laugh, if such a man there be?

Who would not weep, if Atticus were he?

What tho' my Name stood rubric on the walls

Or plaister'd posts, with claps, in capitals?

Or smoking forth, a hundred hawkers' load,5

On wings of winds came flying all abroad?

I sought no homage from the Race that write;

I kept, like Asian Monarchs, from their sight:

Poems I heeded (now be-rhym'd so long)

No more than thou, great George! a birth-day song.

I ne'er with wits or witlings pass'd my days,

To spread about the itch of verse and praise;

Nor like a puppy, daggled thro' the town,

To fetch and carry sing-song up and down;

Nor at Rehearsals sweat, and mouth'd, and cry'd,

With handkerchief and orange at my side;

But sick of fops, and poetry, and prate,

To Bufo left the whole Castalian state.

Proud as Apollo on his forked hill,

Sat full-blown Bufo, puff'd by ev'ry quill;

Fed with soft Dedication all day long.

Horace and he went hand in hand in song.

His Library (where busts of Poets dead

And a true Pindar stood without a head,)

Receiv'd of wits an undistinguish'd race,

Who first his judgment ask'd, and then a place:

Much they extoll'd his pictures, much his seat,

And flatter'd ev'ry day, and some days eat:

Till grown more frugal in his riper days,

He paid some bards with port, and some with praise;

To some a dry rehearsal saw assign'd,

And others (harder still) he paid in kind.

Dryden alone (what wonder?) came not nigh,

Dryden alone escap'd this judging eye:

But still the Great have kindness in reserve,

He help'd to bury whom he help'd to starve.

May some choice patron bless each gray goose quill!

May ev'ry Bavius have his Bufo still!

So, when a Statesman wants a day's defence,

Or Envy holds a whole week's war with Sense,

Or simple pride for flatt'ry makes demands,

May dunce by dunce be whistled off my hands!

Blest be the Great! for those they take away.

And those they left me; for they left me Gay;

Left me to see neglected Genius bloom,

Neglected die, and tell it on his tomb:

Of all thy blameless life the sole return

My Verse, and Queenb'ry weeping o'er thy urn.

Oh let me live my own, and die so too!

(To live and die is all I have to do:)

Maintain a Poet's dignity and ease,

And see what friends, and read what books I please;

Above a Patron, tho' I condescend

Sometimes to call a minister my friend.

I was not born for Courts or great affairs;

I pay my debts, believe, and say my pray'rs;

Can sleep without a Poem in my head;

Nor know, if Dennis be alive or dead.

Why am I ask'd what next shall see the light?

Heav'ns! was I born for nothing but to write?

Has Life no joys for me? or, (to be grave)

Have I no friend to serve, no soul to save?

"I found him close with Swift" — 'Indeed? no doubt,'

(Cries prating Balbus) 'something will come out.'

'Tis all in vain, deny it as I will.

'No, such a Genius never can lie still;'

And then for mine obligingly mistakes

The first Lampoon Sir Will, or Bubo makes.

Poor guiltless I! and can I choose but smile,

When ev'ry Coxcomb knows me by my Style?

Curst be the verse, how well soe'er it flow,

That tends to make one worthy man my foe,

Give Virtue scandal, Innocence a fear,

Or from the soft-eyed Virgin steal a tear!

But he who hurts a harmless neighbour's peace,

Insults fall'n worth, or Beauty in distress,

Who loves a Lie, lame slander helps about,

Who writes a Libel, or who copies out:

That Fop, whose pride affects a patron's name,

Yet absent, wounds an author's honest fame:

Who can your merit selfishly approve,

And show the sense of it without the love;

Who has the vanity to call you friend,

Yet wants the honour, injur'd, to defend;

Who tells whate'er you think, whate'er you say,

And, if he lie not, must at least betray:

Who to the Dean, and silver bell can swear,

And sees at Canons what was never there;

Who reads, but with a lust to misapply,

Make Satire a Lampoon, and Fiction, Lie.

A lash like mine no honest man shall dread,

But all such babbling blockheads in his stead.

Let Sporus tremble — A. What? that thing of silk,

Sporus, that mere white curd of Ass's milk?

Satire or sense, alas! can Sporus feel?

Who breaks a butterfly upon a wheel?

P. Yet let me flap this bug with gilded wings,

This painted child of dirt, that stinks and stings;

Whose buzz the witty and the fair annoys,

Yet wit ne'er tastes, and beauty ne'er enjoys:

So well-bred spaniels civilly delight

In mumbling of the game they dare not bite.

Eternal smiles his emptiness betray,

As shallow streams run dimpling all the way.

Whether in florid impotence he speaks,

And, as the prompter breathes, the puppet squeaks;

Or at the ear of Eve, familiar Toad,

Half froth, half venom, spits himself abroad,

In puns, or politics, or tales, or lies,

Or spite, or smut, or rhymes, or blasphemies.

(His wit all see-saw, between that and this,

(Now high, now low, now master up, now miss,

(And he himself one vile Antithesis.

Amphibious thing! that acting either part,

The trifling head or the corrupted heart,

Fop at the toilet, flatt'rer at the board,

Now trips a Lady, and now struts a Lord.

Eve's tempter thus the Rabbins have exprest,

A Cherub's face, a reptile all the rest;

Beauty that shocks you, parts that none will trust;

Wit that can creep, and pride that licks the dust.

Not Fortune's worshipper, nor fashion's fool,

Not Lucre's madman, nor Ambition's tool,

Not proud, nor servile; — be one Poet's praise,

That, if he pleas'd, he pleas'd by manly ways:

That Flatt'ry, ev'n to Kings, he held a shame,

And thought a Lie in verse or prose the same.

That not in Fancy's maze he wander'd long,

But stoop'd to Truth, and moraliz'd his song:

That not for Fame, but Virtue's better end,

He stood the furious foe, the timid friend,

The damning critic, half approving wit,

The coxcomb hit, or fearing to be hit;

Laugh'd at the loss of friends he never had,

The dull, the proud, the wicked, and the mad;

The distant threats of vengeance on his head,

The blow unfelt, the tear he never shed;

The tale reviv'd, the lie so oft o'erthrown,

Th' imputed trash, and dulness not his own;

The morals blacken'd when the writings scape,

The libell'd person, and the pictur'd shape;

Abuse, on all he lov'd, or lov'd him, spread,

A friend in exile, or a father, dead;

The whisper, that to greatness still too near,

Perhaps, yet vibrates on his Sov'reign's ear: —

Welcome for thee, fair Virtue! all the past;

For thee, fair Virtue! welcome ev'n the last!

A. But why insult the poor, affront the great?

P. A knave's a knave, to me, in ev'ry state:

Alike my scorn, if he succeed or fail,

Sporus at court, or Japhet in a jail

A hireling scribbler, or a hireling peer,

Knight of the post corrupt, or of the shire;

If on a Pillory, or near a Throne,

He gain his Prince's ear, or lose his own.

Yet soft by nature, more a dupe than wit,

Sappho can tell you how this man was bit;

This dreaded Sat'rist Dennis will confess

Foe to his pride, but friend to his distress:

So humble, he has knock'd at Tibbald's door,

Has drunk with Cibber, nay has rhym'd for Moore.

Full ten years slander'd, did he once reply?

Three thousand suns went down on Welsted's lie.

To please a Mistress one aspers'd his life;

He lash'd him not, but let her be his wife.

Let Budgel charge low Grubstreet on his quill,

And write whate'er he pleas'd, except his Will;

Let the two Curlls of Town and Court, abuse

His father, mother, body, soul, and muse.

Yet why? that Father held it for a rule,

It was a sin to call our neighbour fool:

That harmless Mother thought no wife a whore:

Hear this, and spare his family, James Moore!

Unspotted names, and memorable long!

If there be force in Virtue, or in Song.

Of gentle blood (part shed in Honour's cause.

While yet in Britain Honour had applause)

Each parent sprung — A. What fortune, pray? — P. Their own,

And better got, than Bestia's from the throne.

Born to no Pride, inheriting no Strife,

Nor marrying Discord in a noble wife,

Stranger to civil and religious rage,

The good man walk'd innoxious thro' his age.

Nor Courts he saw, no suits would ever try,

Nor dar'd an Oath, nor hazarded a Lie.

Un-learn'd, he knew no schoolman's subtle art,

No language, but the language of the heart.

By Nature honest, by Experience wise,

Healthy by temp'rance, and by exercise;

His life, tho' long, to sickness past unknown,

His death was instant, and without a groan.

O grant me, thus to live, and thus to die!

Who sprung from Kings shall know less joy than I.

O Friend! may each domestic bliss be thine!

Be no unpleasing Melancholy mine:

Me, let the tender office long engage,

To rock the cradle of reposing Age,

With lenient arts extend a Mother's breath,

Make Languor smile, and smooth the bed of Death,

Explore the thought, explain the asking eye,

And keep a while one parent from the sky!

On cares like these if length of days attend,

May Heav'n, to bless those days, preserve my friend,

Preserve him social, cheerful, and serene,

And just as rich as when he serv'd a Queen.

A. Whether that blessing be deny'd or giv'n,

Thus far was right, the rest belongs to Heav'n.

5

10

15

20

25

30

35

40

45

50

55

60

65

70

75

80

85

90

95

100

105

110

115

120

125

130

135

140

145

150

155

160

165

170

175

180

185

190

195

200

205

210

215

220

225

230

235

240

245

250

255

260

265

270

275

280

285

290

295

300

305

310

315

320

325

330

335

340

345

350

355

360

365

370

375

380

385

390

395

400

405

410

415

Contents

Ode on Solitude

Happy the man whose wish and care

A few paternal acres bound,

Content to breathe his native air,

In his own ground.

Whose herds with milk, whose fields with bread,

Whose flocks supply him with attire,

Whose trees in summer yield him shade,

In winter fire.

Blest, who can unconcern'dly find

Hours, days, and years slide soft away,

In health of body, peace of mind,

Quiet by day,

Sound sleep by night; study and ease,

Together mixt; sweet recreation;

And Innocence, which most does please

With meditation.

Thus let me live, unseen, unknown,

Thus unlamented let me die,

Steal from the world, and not a stone

Tell where I lie.

5

10

15

20

Contents

The Descent of Dullness

from The Dunciad, Book IV.

In vain, in vain — the all-composing Hour

Resistless falls: the Muse obeys the Pow'r.

She comes! she comes! the sable Throne behold

Of Night primæval and of Chaos old!

Before her, Fancy's gilded clouds decay,

And all its varying Rain-bows die away.

Wit shoots in vain its momentary fires,

The meteor drops, and in a flash expires.

As one by one, at dread Medea's strain,

The sick'ning stars fade off th' ethereal plain;

As Argus' eyes by Hermes' wand opprest,

Clos'd one by one to everlasting rest;

Thus at her felt approach, and secret might,

Art after Art goes out, and all is Night.

See skulking Truth to her old cavern fled,

Mountains of Casuistry heap'd o'er her head!

Philosophy, that lean'd on Heav'n before,

Shrinks to her second cause, and is no more.

Physic of Metaphysic begs defence,

And Metaphysic calls for aid on Sense!

See Mystery to Mathematics fly!

In vain! they gaze, turn giddy, rave, and die.

Religion blushing veils her sacred fires,

And unawares Morality expires.

For public Flame, nor private, dares to shine;

Nor human Spark is left, nor Glimpse divine!

Lo! thy dread Empire, Chaos! is restor'd;

Light dies before thy uncreating word;

Thy hand, great Anarch! lets the curtain fall,

And universal Darkness buries All.

5

10

15

20

25

30

Contents

Epitaph on Gay

In Westminster Abbey, 1732

Of Manners gentle, of Affections mild;

In Wit, a Man; Simplicity, a Child:

With native Humour temp'ring virtuous Rage,

Form'd to delight at once and lash the age:

Above Temptation, in a low Estate,

And uncorrupted, ev'n among the Great:

A safe Companion, and an easy Friend,

Unblam'd thro' Life, lamented in thy End.

These are Thy Honours! not that here thy Bust

Is mix'd with Heroes, or with Kings thy dust;

But that the Worthy and the Good shall say,

Striking their pensive bosoms — Here lies Gay.

5

10

Contents

Notes on The Rape of the Lock

Introduction

In 1711 Pope, who had just published his Essay on Criticism, was looking about for new worlds to conquer. A fortunate chance threw in his way a subject exactly suited to his tastes and powers. He seized upon it, dashed off his first sketch in less than a fortnight, and published it anonymously in a Miscellany issued by Lintot in 1712. But the theme had taken firm root in his mind. Dissatisfied with his first treatment of it, he determined, against the advice of the best critic of the day, to recast the work, and lift it from a mere society jeu d'esprit into an elaborate mock-heroic poem. He did so and won a complete success. Even yet, however, he was not completely satisfied and from time to time he added a touch to his work until he finally produced the finished picture which we know as The Rape of the Lock. As it stands, it is an almost flawless masterpiece, a brilliant picture and light-hearted mockery of the gay society of Queen Anne's day, on the whole the most satisfactory creation of Pope's genius, and, perhaps, the best example of the mock-heroic in any literature.

The occasion which gave rise to The Rape of the Lock has been so often related that it requires only a brief restatement. Among the Catholic families of Queen Anne's day, who formed a little society of their own, Miss Arabella Fermor was a reigning belle. In a youthful frolic which overstepped the bounds of propriety Lord Petre, a young nobleman of her acquaintance, cut off a lock of her hair. The lady was offended, the two families took up the quarrel, a lasting estrangement, possibly even a duel, was threatened. At this juncture a common friend of the two families, a Mr. Caryll, nephew of a well-known Jacobite exile for whom he is sometimes mistaken, suggested to Pope "to write a poem to make a jest of it," and so kill the quarrel with laughter. Pope consented, wrote his first draft of The Rape of the Lock, and passed it about in manuscript. Pope says himself that it had its effect in the two families; certainly nothing more is heard of the feud. How Miss Fermor received the poem is a little uncertain. Pope complains in a letter written some months after the poem had appeared in print that "the celebrated lady is offended." According to Johnson she liked the verses well enough to show them to her friends, and a niece of hers said years afterward that Mr. Pope's praise had made her aunt "very troublesome and conceited." It is not improbable that Belinda was both flattered and offended. Delighted with the praise of her beauty she may none the less have felt called upon to play the part of the offended lady when the poem got about and the ribald wits of the day began to read into it double meanings which reflected upon her reputation. To soothe her ruffled feelings Pope dedicated the second edition of the poem to her in a delightful letter in which he thanked her for having permitted the publication of the first edition to forestall an imperfect copy offered to a bookseller, declared that the character of Belinda resembled her in nothing but in beauty, and affirmed that he could never hope that his poem should pass through the world half so uncensured as she had done. It would seem that the modern critics who have undertaken to champion Miss Fermor against what they are pleased to term the revolting behavior of the poet are fighting a needless battle. A pretty girl who would long since have been forgotten sat as an unconscious model to a great poet; he made her the central figure in a brilliant picture and rendered her name immortal. That is the whole story, and when carping critics begin to search the poem for the improprieties of conduct to which they say Pope alluded, one has but to answer in Pope's own words.

If to her share some female errors fall,

Look on her face, and you'll forget 'em all.

Pope's statement in the dedication that he had been forced into publishing the first draft of the poem before his design of enlarging it was half executed is probably to be taken, like many of his statements, with a sufficient grain of salt. Pope had a curious habit of protesting that he was forced into publishing his letters, poems, and other trifles, merely to forestall the appearance of unauthorized editions. It is more likely that it was the undoubted success of The Rape of the Lock in its first form which gave him the idea of working up the sketch into a complete mock-heroic poem.

Examples of such a poem were familiar enough to Pope. Not to go back to the pseudo-Homeric mock epic which relates the battle of the frogs and mice, Vida in Italy and Boileau in France, with both of whom Pope, as the Essay on Criticism shows, was well acquainted, had done work of this kind. Vida's description of the game of chess in his Scacchia Ludus certainly gave him the model for the game of ombre in the third canto of The Rape of the Lock; Boileau's Lutrin probably suggested to him the idea of using the mock-heroic for the purposes of satire.

Now it was a dogma of the critical creed of the day, which Pope devoutly accepted, that every epic must have a well-recognized "machinery." Machinery, as he kindly explained to Miss Fermor, was a "term invented by the critics to signify that part which the deities, angels, or demons are made to act in a poem," in short for the whole supernatural element. Such machinery was quite wanting in the first draft of the Rape; it must be supplied if the poem was to be a true epic, even of the comic kind. And the machinery must be of a nature which would lend itself to the light satiric tone of the poem. What was it to be? The employment of what we may call Christian machinery, the angels and devils of Tasso and Milton, was, of course, out of the question. The employment of the classic machinery was almost as impossible. It would have been hard for such an admirer of the classics as Pope to have taken the deities of Olympus otherwise than seriously. And even if he had been able to treat them humorously, the humor would have been a form of burlesque quite at variance with what he had set out to accomplish. For Pope's purpose, springing naturally from the occasion which set him to writing the Rape, was not to burlesque what was naturally lofty by exhibiting it in a degraded light, but to show the true littleness of the trivial by treating it in a grandiose and mock-heroic fashion, to make the quarrel over the stolen lock ridiculous by raising it to the plane of the epic contest before the walls of Troy.

In his perplexity a happy thought, little less in fact than an inspiration of genius, came to Pope. He had been reading a book by a clever French abbé treating in a satiric fashion of the doctrines of the so-called Rosicrucians, in particular of their ideas of elemental spirits and the influence of these spirits upon human affairs. Here was the machinery he was looking for made to his hand. There would be no burlesque in introducing the Rosicrucian sylphs and gnomes into a mock-heroic poem, for few people, certainly not the author of the Comte de Gabalis, took them seriously. Yet the widespread popularity of this book, to say nothing of the existence of certain Rosicrucian societies, had rendered their names familiar to the society for which Pope wrote. He had but to weave them into the action of his poem, and the brilliant little sketch of society was transformed into a true mock-epic.

The manner in which this interweaving was accomplished is one of the most satisfactory evidences of Pope's artistic genius. He was proud of it himself. "The making the machinery, and what was published before, hit so well together, is," he told Spencer, "I think, one of the greatest proofs of judgment of anything I ever did." And he might well be proud. Macaulay, in a well-known passage, has pointed out how seldom in the history of literature such a recasting of a poem has been successfully accomplished. But Pope's revision of The Rape of the Lock was so successful that the original form was practically done away with. No one reads it now but professed students of the literature of Queen Anne's time. And so artfully has the new matter been woven into the old that if the recasting of The Rape of the Lock were not a commonplace even in school histories of English literature, not one reader in a hundred would suspect that the original sketch had been revised and enlarged to more than twice its length. It would be an interesting task for the student to compare the two forms printed in this edition, to note exactly what has been added, and the reasons for its addition, and to mark how Pope has smoothed the junctures and blended the old and the new. Nothing that he could do would admit him more intimately to the secrets of Pope's mastery of his art.

A word must be said in closing as to the merits of The Rape of the Lock and its position in English literature. In the first place it is an inimitable picture of one phase, at least, of the life of the time, of the gay, witty, heartless society of Queen Anne's day. Slowly recovering from the licentious excesses of the Restoration, society at this time was perhaps unmoral rather than immoral. It was quite without ideals, unless indeed the conventions of "good form" may be dignified by that name. It lacked the brilliant enthusiasm of Elizabethan times as well as the religious earnestness of the Puritans and the devotion to patriotic and social ideals which marked a later age. Nothing, perhaps, is more characteristic of the age than its attitude toward women. It affected indeed a tone of high-flown adoration which thinly veiled a cynical contempt. It styled woman a goddess and really regarded her as little better than a doll. The passion of love had fallen from the high estate it once possessed and become the mere relaxation of the idle moments of a man of fashion.

In the comedies of Congreve, for example, a lover even if honestly in love thinks it as incumbent upon him to make light of his passion before his friends as to exaggerate it in all the forms of affected compliment before his mistress.

In The Rape of the Lock Pope has caught and fixed forever the atmosphere of this age. It is not the mere outward form and circumstance, the manners and customs, the patching, powdering, ogling, gambling, of the day that he has reproduced, though his account of these would alone suffice to secure the poem immortality as a contribution to the history of society. The essential spirit of the age breathes from every line. No great English poem is at once so brilliant and so empty, so artistic, and yet so devoid of the ideals on which all high art rests. It is incorrect, I think, to consider Pope in The Rape of the Lock as the satirist of his age. He was indeed clever enough to perceive its follies, and witty enough to make sport of them, but it is much to be doubted whether he was wise enough at this time to raise his eyes to anything better. In the social satires of Pope's great admirer, Byron, we are at no loss to perceive the ideal of personal liberty which the poet opposes to the conventions he tears to shreds. Is it possible to discover in The Rape of the Lock any substitute for Belinda's fancies and the Baron's freaks? The speech of Clarissa which Pope inserted as an afterthought to point the moral of the poem recommends Belinda to trust to merit rather than to charms. But "merit" is explicitly identified with good humor, a very amiable quality, but hardly of the highest rank among the moral virtues. And the avowed end and purpose of "merit" is merely to preserve what beauty gains, the flattering attentions of the other sex, — surely the lowest ideal ever set before womankind. The truth is, I think, that The Rape of the Lock represents Pope's attitude toward the social life of his time in the period of his brilliant youth. He was at once dazzled, amused, and delighted by the gay world in which he found himself. The apples of pleasure had not yet turned to ashes on his lips, and it is the poet's sympathy with the world he paints which gives to the poem the air, most characteristic of the age itself, of easy, idle, unthinking gayety. We would not have it otherwise. There are sermons and satires in abundance in English literature, but there is only one Rape of the Lock.

The form of the poem is in perfect correspondence with its spirit. There is an immense advance over the Essay on Criticism in ease, polish, and balance of matter and manner. And it is not merely in matters of detail that the supremacy of the latter poem is apparent.

The Rape of the Lock is remarkable among all Pope's longer poems as the one complete and perfect whole. It is no mosaic of brilliant epigrams, but an organic creation. It is impossible to detach any one of its witty paragraphs and read it with the same pleasure it arouses when read in its proper connection. Thalestris' call to arms and Clarissa's moral reproof are integral parts of the poem. And as a result, perhaps, of its essential unity The Rape of the Lock bears witness to the presence of a power in Pope that we should hardly have suspected from his other works, the power of dramatic characterization. Elsewhere he has shown himself a master of brilliant portraiture, but Belinda, the Baron, and Thalestris are something more than portraits. They are living people, acting and speaking with admirable consistency. Even the little sketch of Sir Plume is instinct with life.

Finally The Rape of the Lock, in its limitations and defects, no less than in its excellencies, represents a whole period of English poetry, the period which reaches with but few exceptions from Dryden to Wordsworth. The creed which dominated poetic composition during this period is discussed in the introduction to the Essay on Criticism, and is admirably illustrated in that poem itself. Its repression of individuality, its insistence upon the necessity of following in the footsteps of the classic poets, and of checking the outbursts of imagination by the rules of common sense, simply incapacitated the poets of the period from producing works of the highest order. And its insistence upon man as he appeared in the conventional, urban society of the day as the one true theme of poetry, its belief that the end of poetry was to instruct and improve either by positive teaching or by negative satire, still further limited its field. One must remember in attempting an estimate of The Rape of the Lock that it was composed with an undoubting acceptance of this creed and within all these narrowing limitations. And when this is borne in mind, it is hardly too much to say that the poem attains the highest point possible. In its treatment of the supernatural it is as original as a poem could be at that day. The brilliancy of its picture of contemporary society could not be heightened by a single stroke. Its satire is swift and keen, but never ill natured. And the personality of Pope himself shines through every line. Johnson advised authors who wished to attain a perfect style to give their days and nights to a study of Addison. With equal justice one might advise students who wish to catch the spirit of our so-called Augustan age, and to realize at once the limitations and possibilities of its poetry, to devote themselves to the study of The Rape of the Lock.

line

referenc

e

meanin

g

Dedication

Mrs.

Arabella   the title
of Mrs. was still given in Pope's time to unmarried ladies as soon as they were old enough to enter society.

the

Rosicrucian doctrine   the first
mention of the Rosicrucians is in a book published in Germany in 1614, inviting all scholars to join the ranks of a secret society said

to have been founded two centuries before by a certain Christian Rosenkreuz who had mastered the hidden wisdom of the East. It seems probable that this book was an elaborate hoax, but it was taken seriously at the time, and the seventeenth century saw the formation of numerous groups of "Brothers of the Rosy Cross." They dabbled in alchemy, spiritualism, and magic, and mingled modern science with superstitions handed down from ancient times. Pope probably knew nothing more of them than what he had read in Le Comte de Gabalis.

This was the work of a French abbé, de Montfaucon Villars (1635-1673), who was well known in his day both as a preacher and a man of letters. It is really a satire upon the fashionable mystical studies, but treats in a tone of pretended seriousness of secret sciences, of elemental spirits, and of their intercourse with men. It was translated into English in 1680 and again in 1714.

Canto I

1-2

Pope opens his mock-epic with the usual epic formula, the statement of the subject. Compare the first lines of the Iliad, the Æneid, and Paradise Lost. In l. 7 he goes on to call upon the "goddess," i.e. the muse, to relate the cause of the rape. This, too, is an epic formula. Compare Æneid, I, 8, and Paradise Lost, I, 27-33.

3

Caryl

see Introduction. In accordance with his wish his name was not printed in the editions of the poem that came out in Pope's lifetime, appearing there only as C —— — or C —— —l.

4   Belinda
                                                                              a name
used by Pope to denote Miss Fermor, the heroine of The Rape of
the Lock

12   This
line is almost a translation of a line in the Æneid (I, 11), where
Virgil asks if it be possible that such fierce passions (as Juno's)
should exist in the minds of gods.

13   Sol a
good instance of the fondness which Pope shared with most poets
of his time for giving classical names to objects of nature. This
trick was supposed to adorn and elevate poetic diction. Try to find
other instances of this in The Rape of the Lock.

                                                                              Why is
the sun's ray called "tim'rous"?

16   It
was an old convention that lovers were so troubled by their passion
that they could not sleep. In the Prologue to the Canterbury Tales
(ll. 97-98), Chaucer says of the young squire:

So hote he lovede, that by nightertale

He sleep namore than dooth a nightingale.

Pope, of course, is laughing at the easy-going lovers of his day who in spite of their troubles sleep very comfortably till noon.

17   The
lady on awaking rang a little hand-bell that stood on a table by her
bed to call her maid. Then as the maid did not appear at once she
tapped impatiently on the floor with the heel of her slipper. The
watch in the next line was a repeater.

19   All
the rest of this canto was added in the second edition of the poem.
See pp. 84-86. Pope did not notice that he describes Belinda as
waking in I. 14 and still asleep and dreaming in II. 19-116.

20

            guardia
n Sylph

            compar
e ll. 67-78

23   a Birth-
night Beau   a fine
gentleman in his best clothes, such as he would wear at a ball on
the occasion of a royal birthday.

30   The
nurse would have told Belinda the old tales of fairies who danced
by moonlight on rings in the greensward, and dropped silver coins
into the shoes of tidy little maids. The priest, on the other hand,
would have repeated to her the legend of St. Cecilia and her
guardian angel who once appeared in bodily form to her husband
holding two rose garlands gathered in Paradise, or of St. Dorothea,
who sent an angel messenger with a basket of heavenly fruits and
flowers to convert the pagan Theophilus.

42   militia

used here in the general sense of "soldiery."

44 the box in the theater.

the ring the drive in Hyde Park, where the ladies of society took the air.

46 a chair a sedan chair in which ladies used to be carried about. Why is Belinda told to scorn it?

50 What is the meaning of "vehicles" in this line?

56 Ombre the fashionable game of cards in Pope's day. See his account of a game in Canto III and the notes on that passage.

57-67 See Introduction

69-70 Compare Paradise Lost, I, 423-431.

79 conscious of their face: proud of their beauty.

81   These the
gnomes who urge the vain beauties to disdain all offers of love and
play the part of prudes.

85   garters,
stars, and coronets   the
garter is the badge of the Knights of the Garter, an order founded
by Edward III, to which only noble princes and noblemen of the
highest rank were admitted. "Stars" are the jeweled decorations
worn by members of other noble orders. "Coronets" are the inferior
crowns worn by princes and nobles, not by sovereigns.

86   "Your
Grace"   the title
bestowed in England on a duchess — The idea in this passage, ll.
83-86, is that the gnomes fill the girls' minds with hopes of a
splendid marriage and so induce them to "deny love."

94

         imperti
nence

         purpose
less flirtation.

97-98   Florio
... Damon   poetic
names for fine gentlemen; no special individuals are meant.

100

         Why is
a woman's heart called a "toy-shop"?

101   Sword-
knots   tassels

worn at the hilts of swords. In Pope's day every gentleman carried a sword, and these sword-knots were often very gay.

105   who thy
protection claim   what is
the exact meaning of his phrase?

108   thy
ruling Star   the star
that controls thy destinies, a reference to the old belief in astrology.

115   Shock
                                                         Belinda'
s pet dog. His name would seem to show that he was a rough-haired terrier.

118
                                                         Does
this line mean that Belinda had never seen a billet-doux before?

119
                                                         Wounds
, Charms, and Ardors   the
usual language of a love-letter at this time.

124   the
Cosmetic pow'rs   the
deities that preside over a lady's toilet. Note the playful satire with which Pope describes Belinda's toilet as if it were a religious ceremony. Who is "th' inferior priestess" in l. 127?

131   nicely
                                                         carefull
y.

134   Arabia

famous

for its perfumes.

145
set the

head
arrange

the head-dress.

147
Betty
Belinda'

s maid.

Canto II

4
Launch'

d
embark

ed

25
springes
snares

26
the

finny prey
a

characteristic instance of Pope's preference or circumlocution to a direct phrase.

35-36
A

regular formula in classical epics. In Virgil (XI, 794-795) Phœbus grants part of the prayer of Arruns; the other part he scatters to the light winds.

38
vast

French Romances
these

romances were the customary reading of society in Pope's day when there were as yet no English novels. Some of them were of enormous length. Addison found several of them in a typical lady's library, great folio volumes, finely bound in gilt (Spectator, 37).

58   All but
the Sylph   so in
Homer (1-25), while all the rest of the army is sleeping Agamemnon is disturbed by fear of the doom impending over the Greeks at the hands of Hector.

60   Waft
      wave,

or flutter.

70

      Superio
r by the head   so in
Homer (Iliad, III, 225-227) Ajax is described as towering over the other Greeks by head and shoulders.

73   sylphids
      a
feminine form of "sylphs."

74   This
formal opening of Ariel's address to his followers is a parody of a passage in Paradise Lost, V, 600-601.

75   spheres
      either
"worlds" or in a more general sense "regions."

79

      What
are the "wandering orbs," and how do they differ from planets in l.

80?

97
a wash
a lotion
for the complexion.

105
Diana,
the virgin huntress, was in a peculiar sense the goddess of chastity.

106 China
jar the taste
for collecting old china was comparatively new in England at this
time. It had been introduced from Holland by Queen Anne's sister,
Queen Mary, and was eagerly caught up by fashionable society.

113 The
drops the
diamond earrings.

118 the
Petticoat the
huge hoop skirt which had recently become fashionable. Addison,
in a humorous paper in the Tatler (No. 116), describes one as about
twenty-four yards in circumference.

128 bodkin
a large
needle.

133 rivel'd
an
obsolete raiment of "obrivelled."

133 Ixion
accordi

ng to classical mythology Ixion was punished for his sins by being bound forever upon a whirling wheel.

134   Mill

the mill

in which cakes of chocolate were ground up preparatory to making the beverage.

138   orb in

orb   in

concentric circles.

139   thrid

a

variant form of "thread."

Canto III

3   a

structure

Hampto

n Court, a palace on the Thames, a few miles above London. It was begun by Wolsey, and much enlarged by William III. Queen Anne visited it occasionally, and cabinet meetings were sometimes held there. Pope insinuates (l. 6) that the statesmen who met in these councils were as interested in the conquest of English ladies as of foreign enemies.

8   Tea

was still in Queen Anne's day a luxury confined to the rich. It cost, in 1710, from twelve to twenty-eight shillings per pound.

9   The

heroes and the nymphs   the

boating party which started for Hampton Court in Canto II.

17

Snuff-

taking had just become fashionable at this time. The practice is said to date from 1702, when an English admiral brought back fifty tons of snuff found on board some Spanish ships which he had captured in Vigo Bay.

In the Spectator for August 8, 1711, a mock advertisement is inserted professing to teach "the exercise of the snuff-box according to the most fashionable airs and motions," and in the number for April 4, 1712, Steele protests against "an impertinent custom the fine women have lately fallen into of taking snuff."

22   dine

the

usual dinner hour in Queen Anne's reign was about 3 P.M. Fashionable people dined at 4, or later. This allowed the fashionable lady who rose at noon time to do a little shopping and perform "the long labours of the toilet."

26   two ...

Knights   one of

these was the baron, see l. 66.

27   Ombre

a game

of cards invented in Spain. It takes its name from the Spanish phrase originally used by the player who declared trumps: "Yo soy l'hombre," i. e. I am the man. It could be played by three, five, or nine players, but the usual number was three as here. Each of these received nine cards, and one of them named the trump and thus became the "ombre," who played against the two others. If either of the ombre's opponents took more tricks than the ombre, it was "codille" (1. 92). This meant that the opponent took the stake and the ombre had to replace it for the next hand.

A peculiar feature of ombre is the rank, or value, of the cards. The three best cards were called "matadores," a Spanish word meaning "killers." The first of these matadores was "Spadillio," the ace of spades; the third was "Basto," the ace of clubs. The second, "Manillio," varied according to the suit. If a black suit were declared, Maniilio was the two of trumps; if a red suit, Manillio was the seven of trumps. It is worth noting also that the red aces were inferior to the face cards of their suits except when a red suit was trump.

A brief analysis of the game played on this occasion will clear up the passage and leave the reader free to admire the ingenuity with which Pope has described the contest in terms of epic poetry.

Belinda declares spades trumps and so becomes the "ombre." She leads one after the other the three matadores; and takes three tricks. She then leads the next highest card, the king of spades, and wins a fourth trick. Being out of trumps she now leads the king of clubs; but the baron, who has actually held more spades than Belinda, trumps it with the queen of spades. All the trumps are now exhausted and the baron's long suit of diamonds is established. He takes the sixth, seventh, and eighth tricks with the king, queen, and knave of diamonds, respectively. Everything now depends on the last trick, since Belinda and the baron each have taken four. The baron leads the ace of hearts and Belinda takes it with the king, thus escaping "codille" and winning the stake.

30   the
sacred nine   the nine
Muses.

41   succint
      tucked

up.

54   one
Plebeian card   one of
Belinda's opponents is now out of trumps and discards a low card on her lead.

61   Pam
      a term
applied to the knave of clubs which was always the highest card in Lu, another popular game of that day.

74   the
globe   the
jeweled ball which forms one of the regalia of a monarch. The aspect of playing cards has changed not a little since Pope's day, but the globe is still to be seen on the king of clubs.

79   Clubs,
Diamonds, Hearts   these
are the losing cards played by Belinda and the third player on the baron's winning diamonds.

99

      Pope's
old enemy, Dennis, objected to the impropriety of Belinda's filling the sky with exulting shouts, and some modern critics have been

foolish enough to echo his objection. The whole scene is a masterpiece of the mock-heroic. The game is a battle, the cards are warriors, and Belinda's exclamations of pleasure at winning are in the same fashion magnified into the cheers of a victorious army.

100 **canals** the long canals which run through the splendid gardens of Hampton Court, laid out by William III in the Dutch fashion.

106 **berries crackle** The it would seem from this phrase that coffee was at that time roasted as well as ground in the drawing-room. In a letter written shortly after the date of this poem Pope describes Swift as roasting coffee "with his own hands in an engine made for that purpose."

Coffee had been introduced into England about the middle of the seventeenth century. In 1657 a barber who had opened one of the first coffeehouses in London was indicted for "making and selling a sort of liquor called coffee, as a great nuisance and prejudice of the neighborhood." In Pope's time there were nearly three thousand coffee-houses in London.

mill The the coffee-mill.

107 **of Japan** Altars japanned stands for the lamps.

117-118 The

parenthesis in these lines contains a hit at the would-be omniscient politicians who haunted the coffee-houses of Queen Anne's day, and who professed their ability to see through all problems of state with their eyes half-shut. Pope jestingly attributes their wisdom to the inspiring power of coffee.

122   Scylla
                                                                            the
daughter of King Nisus in Grecian legends. Nisus had a purple hair and so long as it was untouched he was unconquerable. Scylla fell in love with one of his enemies and pulled out the hair while Nisus slept. For this crime she was turned into a bird. The story is told in full in Ovid's Metamorphoses, Bk. VIII.

127   Clarissa
                                                                            it does
not appear that Pope had any individual lady in mind. We do not know, at least, that any lady instigated or aided Lord Petre to cut off the lock.

144   An
earthly Lover   we
know nothing of any love affair of Miss Fermor's. Pope mentions the "earthly lover" here to account for Ariel's desertion of Belinda, for he could only protect her so long as she "rejected mankind"; compare Canto I, ll. 67-68.

147   Forfex
                                                                            a Latin
word meaning scissors.

152

                                                                            Pope
borrowed this idea from Milton, who represents the wound inflicted on Satan, by the Archangel Michael as healing

immediately:

Th' ethereal substance closed

Not long divisible.

Paradise Lost, VI, 330-331.

165

Atalantis The

New Atalantis, a four-volume "cornucopia of scandal" involving almost every public character of the day, was published by a Mrs. Manley in 1709. It was very widely read. The Spectator found it, along with a key which revealed the identities of its characters, in the lady's library already mentioned (Spectator, No. 37).

166 the
small pillow a richly
decorated pillow which fashionable ladies used to prop them up in bed when they received morning visits from gentlemen. Addison gives an account of such a visit in the Spectator, No. 45.

167 solemn
days days of
marriage or mourning, on which at this time formal calls were paid.

173 the
labour of the gods the
walls of Troy built by Apollo and Neptune for King Laomedon.

178

unresist
ed
irresisti
ble.

Canto IV

8 Cynthia
a
fanciful name for any fashionable lady. No individual is meant.

mantea
u a loose
upper garment for women.

16 Spleen
the
word is used here as a personification of melancholy, or low
spirits. It was not an uncommon affectation in England at this time.
A letter to the Spectator, No. 53, calls it "the distemper of the great
and the polite."

17 the
Gnome
Umbriel
, who in accordance with his nature now proceeds to stir up
trouble. Compare Canto I, ll. 63-64.

20 The
bitter east wind which put every one into a bad humor was
supposed to be one of the main causes of the spleen.

23 She the
goddess of the spleen. Compare l. 79.

84   Megrim headach
e.

29   store a large
supply.

38   night-
dress   the
modern dressing-gown. The line means that whenever a fashionable beauty bought a new dressing-gown she pretended to be ill in order to show her new possession to sympathetic friends who called on her.

40

                 phanto
ms   these
are the visions, dreadful or delightful, of the disordered imagination produced by spleen.

43   snakes
on rolling spires   like the
serpent which Milton describes in Paradise Lost, IX, 501-502, "erect amidst his circling spires."

46   angels
in machines   angels
coming to help their votaries. The word "machine" here has an old-fashioned technical sense. It was first used to describe the apparatus by which a god was let down upon the stage of the Greek theater. Since a god was only introduced at a critical moment to help the distressed hero, the phrase, "deus ex machina," came to mean a god who rendered aid. Pope transfers it here to angels.

47
throngs

Pope now describes the mad fancies of people so affected by spleen as to imagine themselves transformed to inanimate objects.

51
pipkin
a little

jar. Homer (Iliad, XVIII, 373-377) tells how Vulcan had made twenty wonderful tripods on living wheels that moved from place to place of their own accord.

52
Pope in

a note to this poem says that a lady of his time actually imagined herself to be a goose-pie.

56
A
branch
so

Æneas bore a magic branch to protect him when he descended to the infernal regions (Æneid, VI, 136-143).

Spleen
wort
a sort of

fern which was once supposed to be a remedy against the spleen.

58
the sex
women.

59
vapours
a form

of spleen to which women were supposed to be peculiarly liable, something like our modern hysteria. It seems to have taken its name from the fogs of England which were thought to cause it.

65
a
nymph
Belinda,

who had always been so light-hearted that she had never been a victim of the spleen.

89 **Citron-waters** a liqueur made by distilling brandy with the rind of citrons. It was a fashionable drink for ladies at this time.

71 **Made** men suspicious of their wives.

82 **Ulysses** Homer (Odyssey, X, 1-25) tells how Æolus, the god of the winds, gave Ulysses a wallet of oxhide in which all the winds that might oppose his journey homeward were closely bound up.

89 **Thalestris** the name of a warlike queen of the Amazons. Pope uses it here for a friend of Belinda's, who excites her to revenge herself for the rape of her lock. It is said that this friend was a certain Mrs. Morley.

102 **loads of lead curl** papers used to be fastened with strips of lead.

105 **Honour** female reputation.

109 **toast** a slang term in Pope's day for a reigning beauty whose health was

regularly drunk by her admirers. Steele (Tatler, No. 24) says that the term had its rise from an accident that happened at Bath in the reign of Charles II. A famous beauty was bathing there in public, and one of her admirers filled a glass with the water in which she stood and drank her health.

"There was in the place," says Steele "a gay fellow, half-fuddled, who offered to jump in, and swore though he liked not the liquor, he would have the Toast. He was opposed in his resolution; yet this whim gave foundation to the present honor which is done to the lady we mention in our liquors, who has ever since been called a Toast."

To understand the point of the story one must know that it was an old custom to put a bit of toast in hot drinks.

In this line in the poem Thalestris insinuates that if Belinda submits tamely to the rape of the lock, her position as a toast will be forfeited.

113-116

Thalestris supposes that the baron will have the lock set in a ring under a bit of crystal. Old-fashioned hair-rings of this kind are still to be seen.

117 Hyde-park Circus the Ring of Canto I, l. 44. Grass was not likely to grow there so long as it remained the fashionable place to drive.

118   in the
sound of Bow   within
hearing of the bells of the church of St. Mary le Bow in Cheapside.
So far back as Ben Jonson's time (Eastward Ho, I, ii, 36) it was the
mark of the unfashionable middle-class citizen to live in this
quarter. A "wit" in Queen Anne's day would have scorned to lodge
there.

121   Sir
Plume   this was
Sir George Brown, brother of Mrs. Morley (Thalestris). He was not
unnaturally offended at the picture drawn of him in this poem.
Pope told a friend many years later that

"nobody was angry but Sir George Brown, and he was a good
deal so, and for a long time. He could not bear that Sir Plume
should talk nothing but nonsense."

124   a
clouded cane   a cane
of polished wood with cloudlike markings. In the Tatler, Mr.
Bickerstaff sits in judgment on canes, and takes away a cane,
"curiously clouded, with a transparent amber head, and a blue
ribband to hang upon his wrist," from a young gentleman as a
piece of idle foppery. There are some amusing remarks on the
"conduct" of canes in the same essay.

133   The
baron's oath is a parody of the oath of Achilles (Iliad, I, 234).

142   The
breaking of the bottle of sorrows, etc., is the cause of Belinda's

change of mood from wrath as in l. 93 to tears, 143-144.

155   the gilt
Chariot   the
painted and gilded coach in which ladies took the air in London.

156   Bohea
tea, the
name comes from a range of hills in China where a certain kind of tea was grown.

162   the
patch-box   the box
which held the little bits of black sticking-plaster with which ladies used to adorn their faces. According to Addison (Spectator, No. 81), ladies even went so far in this fad as to patch on one side of the face or the other, according to their politics.

Canto V

5   the
Trojan   Æneas,
who left Carthage in spite of the wrath of Dido and the entreaties of her sister Anna.

7-36   Pope
inserted these lines in a late revision in 1717, in order, as he said, to open more clearly the moral of the poem. The speech of Clarissa is a parody of a famous speech by Sarpedon in the Iliad, XII, 310-328.

14   At
this time the gentlemen always sat in the side boxes of the theater;

the ladies in the front boxes.

20   As
vaccination had not yet been introduced, small-pox was at this time
a terribly dreaded scourge.

23   In
the Spectator, No. 23, there is inserted a mock advertisement,
professing to teach the whole art of ogling, the church ogle, the
playhouse ogle, a flying ogle fit for the ring, etc.

24
                                                                    Painting
the face was a common practice of the belles of this time. The
Spectator, No. 41, contains a bitter attack on the painted ladies
whom it calls the "Picts."

37   virago
                                                                    a fierce,
masculine woman, here used for Thalestris.

45   In
the Iliad (Bk. XX) the gods are represented as taking sides for the
Greeks and Trojans and fighting among themselves. Pallas opposes
Ares, or Mars; and Hermes, Latona.

48
                                                                    Olympu
s   the hill
on whose summit the gods were supposed to dwell, often used for
heaven itself.

50
                                                                    Neptun
e   used
here for the sea over which Neptune presided.

53   a

sconce's height   the top
of an ornamental bracket for holding candles.

61

Explain

the metaphor in this line.

64   The

quotation is from a song in an opera called Camilla.

65   The

Mæander is a river in Asia Minor. Ovid (Heroides, VII, 1-2)
represents the swan as singing his death-song on its banks.

68

Chloe: a

fanciful name. No real person is meant.

71   The

figure of Jove weighing the issue of a battle in his scales is found
in the Iliad, VIII, 69-73. Milton imitated it in Paradise Lost, IX,
996-1004. When the men's wits mounted it showed that they were
lighter, less important, than the lady's hair, and so were destined to
lose the battle.

89-96   This

pedigree of Belinda's bodkin is a parody of Homer's account of
Agamemnon's scepter (Iliad, II, 100-108).

105-106   In

Shakespeare's play Othello fiercely demands to see a handkerchief
which he has given his wife, and takes her inability to show it to
him as a proof of her infidelity.

113   the

lunar sphere: it was an old superstition that everything lost on earth
went to the moon. An Italian poet, Ariosto, uses this notion in a
poem with which Pope was familiar (Orlando Furioso, Canto
XXXIV), and from which he borrowed some of his ideas for the
cave of Spleen.

122   Why
does Pope include "tomes of casuistry" in this collection?

125   There
was a legend that Romulus never died, but had been caught up to
the skies in a storm. Proculus, a Roman senator, said that Romulus
had descended from heaven and spoken to him and then ascended
again (Livy, I, 16).

129   Berenic
e's Locks   :
Berenice was an Egyptian queen who dedicated a lock of hair for
her husband's safe return from war. It was said afterward to have
become a constellation, and a Greek poet wrote some verses on the
marvel.

132   Why
were the Sylphs pleased?

133   the Mall
the
upper side of St. James's park in London, a favorite place at this
time for promenades.

136

Rosamo
nda's lake   a pond
near one of the gates of St. James's park, a favorite rendezvous for
lovers.

137

Partridg
e   an
almanac maker of Pope's day who was given to prophesying future
events. Shortly before this poem was written Swift had issued a
mock almanac foretelling that Partridge would die on a certain day.
When that day came Swift got out a pamphlet giving a full account
of Partridge's death. In spite of the poor man's protests, Swift and
his friends kept on insisting that he was dead. He was still living,
however, when Pope wrote this poem. Why does Pope call him "th'
egregious wizard"?

138

Galileo'
s eyes   the
telescope, first used by the Italian astronomer Galileo.

140

Louis
XIV of France, the great enemy of England at this time.

Rome
here
used to denote the Roman Catholic Church.

143   the
shining sphere   an
allusion to the old notion that all the stars were set in one sphere in
the sky. Belinda's lost lock, now a star, is said to add a new light to
this sphere.

147   What
are the "fair suns"?

Contents

Notes on An Essay on Criticism

Introduction

The Essay on Criticism was the first really important work that Pope gave to the world. He had been composing verses from early boyhood, and had actually published a set of Pastorals which had attracted some attention. He was already known to the literary set of London coffeehouses as a young man of keen wit and high promise, but to the reading public at large he was as yet an unknown quantity. With the appearance of the Essay, Pope not only sprang at once into the full light of publicity, but seized almost undisputed that position as the first of living English poets which he was to retain unchallenged till his death. Even after his death down to the Romantic revival, in fact, Pope's supremacy was an article of critical faith, and this supremacy was in no small measure founded upon the acknowledged merits of the Essay on Criticism. Johnson, the last great representative of Pope's own school of thought in matters literary, held that the poet had never excelled this early work and gave it as his deliberate opinion that if Pope had written nothing else, the Essay would have placed him among the first poets and the first critics. The Essay on Criticism is hardly an epoch-making poem, but it certainly "made" Alexander Pope.

The poem was published anonymously in the spring of 1711, when Pope was twenty-three years old. There has been considerable dispute as to the date of its composition; but the facts seem to be that it was begun in 1707 and finished in 1709 when Pope had it printed, not for publication, but for purposes of further correction. As it stands, therefore, it represents a work planned at the close of Pope's precocious youth, and executed and polished in the first flush of his manhood. And it is quite fair to say that considering the age of its author the Essay on Criticism is one of the most remarkable works in English.

Not that there is anything particularly original about the Essay. On the contrary, it is one of the most conventional of all Pope's works. It has nothing of the lively fancy of The Rape of the Lock, little or nothing of the personal note which stamps the later satires and epistles as so peculiarly Pope's own. Apart from its brilliant epigrammatic expression the Essay on Criticism might have been written by almost any man of letters in Queen Anne's day who took the trouble to think a little about the laws of literature, and who thought about those laws strictly in accordance with the accepted conventions of his time. Pope is not in the least to be blamed for this lack of originality. Profound original criticism is perhaps the very last thing to be expected of a brilliant boy, and Pope was little more when he planned this work. But boy as he was, he had already accomplished an immense amount of desultory reading, not only in literature proper, but in literary criticism as well. He told Spence in later years that in his youth he had gone through all the best critics, naming especially Quintilian, Rapin, and Bossu. A mere cursory reading of the Essay shows that he had also studied Horace, Vida, and Boileau. Before he began to write he had, so he told Spence, "digested all the matter of the poem into prose." In other words, then, the Essay on Criticism is at once the result of Pope's early studies, the embodiment of the received literary doctrines of his age, and, as a consecutive study of his poems shows, the programme in accordance with which, making due allowance for certain exceptions and inconsistencies, he evolved the main body of his work.

It would, however, be a mistake to treat, as did Pope's first editor, the Essay on Criticism as a methodical, elaborate, and systematic treatise. Pope, indeed, was flattered to have a scholar of such recognized authority as Warburton to interpret his works, and permitted him to print a commentary upon the Essay, which is quite as long and infinitely duller than the original. But the true nature of the poem is indicated by its title. It is not an Art of Poetry such as Boileau composed, but an Essay. And by the word "essay," Pope meant exactly what Bacon did, — a tentative sketch, a series of detached thoughts upon a subject, not a complete study or a methodical treatise. All that we know of Pope's method of study, habit of thought, and practice of composition goes to support this opinion. He read widely but desultorily; thought swiftly and brilliantly, but illogically and inconsistently; and composed in minute sections, on the backs of letters and scraps of waste paper, fragments which he afterward united, rather than blended, to make a complete poem, a mosaic, rather than a picture.

Yet the Essay is by no means the "collection of independent maxims tied together by the printer, but having no natural order," which De Quincey pronounced it to be. It falls naturally into three parts. The first deals with the rules derived by classic critics from the practice of great poets, and ever since of binding force both in the composition and in the criticism of poetry. The second analyzes with admirable sagacity the causes of faulty criticism as pride, imperfect learning, prejudice, and so on. The third part discusses the qualities which a true critic should possess, good taste, learning, modesty, frankness, and tact, and concludes with a brief sketch of the history of criticism from Aristotle to Walsh. This is the general outline of the poem, sufficient, I think, to show that it is not a mere bundle of poetic formulæ. But within these broad limits the thought of the poem wanders freely, and is quite rambling, inconsistent, and illogical enough to show that Pope is not formulating an exact and definitely determined system of thought.

Such indeed was, I fancy, hardly his purpose. It was rather to give clear, vivid, and convincing expression to certain ideas which were at that time generally accepted as orthodox in the realm of literary criticism. No better expression of these ideas can be found anywhere than in the Essay itself, but a brief statement in simple prose of some of the most important may serve as a guide to the young student of the essay.

In the first place, the ultimate source alike of poetry and criticism is a certain intuitive faculty, common to all men, though more highly developed in some than others, called Reason, or, sometimes, Good Sense. The first rule for the budding poet or critic is "Follow Nature." This, by the way, sounds rather modern, and might be accepted by any romantic poet. But by "Nature" was meant not at all the natural impulses of the individual, but those rules founded upon the natural and common reason of mankind which the ancient critics had extracted and codified from the practice of the ancient poets. Pope says explicitly "to follow nature is to follow them;" and he praises Virgil for turning aside from his own original conceptions to imitate Homer, for:

Nature and Homer were, he found, the same.

Certain exceptions to these rules were, indeed, allowable, — severer critics than Pope, by the way, absolutely denied this, — but only to the ancient poets. The moderns must not dare to make use of them, or at the very best moderns must only venture upon such exceptions to the rules as classic precedents would justify. Inasmuch as all these rules were discovered and illustrated in ancient times, it followed logically that the great breach with antiquity, which is called the Middle Ages, was a period of hopeless and unredeemed barbarism, incapable of bringing forth any good thing. The light of literature began to dawn again with the revival of learning at the Renaissance, but the great poets of the Renaissance, Spenser and Shakespeare, for example, were "irregular," that is, they trusted too much to their individual powers and did not accept with sufficient humility the orthodox rules of poetry. This dogma, by the way, is hardly touched upon in the Essay, but is elaborated with great emphasis in Pope's later utterance on the principles of literature, the well-known Epistle to Augustus. Finally with the establishment of the reign of Reason in France under Louis XIV, and in England a little later, the full day had come, and literary sins of omission and commission that might be winked at in such an untutored genius as Shakespeare were now unpardonable. This last dogma explains the fact that in the brief sketch of the history of criticism which concludes the Essay, Pope does not condescend to name an English poet or critic prior to the reign of Charles II.

It would be beside the purpose to discuss these ideas to-day or to attempt an elaborate refutation of their claims to acceptance. Time has done its work upon them, and the literary creed of the wits of Queen Anne's day is as antiquated as their periwigs and knee-breeches. Except for purposes of historical investigation it is quite absurd to take the Essay on Criticism seriously.

And yet it has even for us of to-day a real value. Our age absolutely lacks a standard of literary criticism; and of all standards the one least likely to be accepted is that of Pope and his fellow-believers. Individual taste reigns supreme in this democratic age, and one man's judgment is as good as, perhaps a little better than, another's. But even this democratic and individual age may profit by turning back for a time to consider some of the general truths, as valid to-day as ever, to which Pope gave such inimitable expression, or to study the outlines of that noble picture of the true critic which St. Beuve declared every professed critic should frame and hang up in his study. An age which seems at times upon the point of throwing classical studies overboard as useless lumber might do far worse than listen to the eloquent tribute which the poet pays to the great writers of antiquity. And finally nothing could be more salutary for an age in which literature itself has caught something of the taint of the prevailing commercialism than to bathe itself again in that spirit of sincere and disinterested love of letters which breathes throughout the Essay and which, in spite of all his errors, and jealousies, and petty vices, was the master-passion of Alexander Pope.

line

referenc

e

meanin

g

6   censure
the
word has here its original meaning of "judge," not its modern
"judge severely" or "blame."

8

Because
each foolish poem provokes a host of foolish commentators and
critics.

15-16   This
assertion that only a good writer can be a fair critic is not to be
accepted without reservation.

17   wit The
word "wit" has a number of different meanings in this poem, and
the student should be careful to discriminate between them. It
means

mind, intellect, l. 61;

learning, culture, l 727;

imagination, genius, l. 82;

the power to discover amusing analogies, or the apt expression of such an analogy, ll. 449, 297;

a man possessed of wit in its various significations, l. 45;

this last form usually occurs in the plural, ll. 104, 539.

26   the
maze of schools   the
labyrinth of conflicting systems of thought, especially of criticism.

21

                                        coxcom
bs ... fools   what is
the difference in meaning between these words in this passage?

30-31   In
this couplet Pope hits off the spiteful envy of conceited critics toward successful writers. If the critic can write himself, he hates the author as a rival; if he cannot, he entertains against him the deep grudge an incapable man so often cherishes toward an effective worker.

34   Mævius
                                           a
poetaster whose name has been handed down by Virgil and Horace. His name, like that of his associate, Bavius, has become a by-word for a wretched scribbler.

                                        Apollo
                                        here

thought of as the god of poetry. The true poet was inspired by Apollo; but a poetaster like Mævius wrote without inspiration, as it were, in spite of the god.

40-43
Pope here compares "half-learned" critics to the animals which old writers reported were bred from the Nile mud. In Antony and Cleopatra, for example, Lepidus says, "Your serpent of Egypt is bred now of your mud by the operation of your sun; so is your crocodile." Pope thinks of these animals as in the unformed stage, part "kindled into life, part a lump of mud." So these critics are unfinished things for which no proper name can be found. "Equivocal generation" is the old term used to denote spontaneous generation of this sort. Pope applies it here to critics without proper training who spring spontaneously from the mire of ignorance.

44
tell
count

45
The idea is that a vain wit's tongue could out-talk a hundred ordinary men's.

53
pretendi
ng wit
presumi
ng, or ambitious mind.

56-58
memory
... understanding imagination
This is the old threefold division of the human mind. Pope means that where one of these faculties is above the average in any individual, another of them is sure to fall below. Is this always the case?

63   peculiar

arts   special

branches of knowledge.

73   In

what sense can nature be called the source, the end, and the test of art?

76   th'

informing soul

        explana

tion

80-81

        What

two meanings are attached to "wit" in this couplet?

84   'Tis

more   it is

more important.

        the

Muse's steed

        Pegasus

, the winged horse of Greek mythology, was supposed to be the horse of the Muses and came to be considered a symbol of poetic genius.

86   gen'rous

        high-

bred.

88

        What is

the difference between "discovered" and "devised"?

94

Parnass

us' top the

Muses were supposed to dwell on the top of Parnassus, a mountain in Greece. Great poets are here thought of as having climbed the mountain to dwell with the Muses.

96

What is

(cf. text) "the immortal prize"?

99 She i. e.

learned Greece, especially Greek criticism, which obtained the rules of poetry from the practice of great poets, and, as it were, systematized their inspiration.

104

followi

ng wits later

scholars.

105

What is

meant by "the mistress" and "the maid" in this line?

109 Doctor's

bills

prescrip

tions.

112

These

are the prosy commentators on great poets, whose dreary notes often disgust readers with the original.

120 fable

a plot.

123

What is
the difference between "cavil" and "criticise"?

129   the
Mantuan Muse   the
poetry of Virgil, which Pope thinks the best commentary on
Homer. In what sense is this to be understood?

130   Maro
Virgil,
whose full name was Publius Vergilius Maro, Pope here praises
Virgil's well-known imitation of Homer. Since "nature and Homer
were the same," a young poet like Virgil could do nothing better
than copy Homer.

138   the
Stagirite

Aristotl
e, a native of Stagyra, was the first and one of the greatest of
literary critics. His "rules" were drawn from the practice of great
poets, and so, according to Pope, to imitate Homer was to obey the
"ancient rules."

141

There
are some beauties in poetry which cannot be explained by
criticism.

142

happine
ss   used
here to express the peculiar charm of spontaneous poetic

expression as contrasted with "care," 'i.e.' the art of revising and improving, which can be taught.

152   vulgar
bounds   the
limitations imposed upon ordinary writers.

157   out of ...
rise   surpass
the ordinary scenes of nature.

159   Great
wits   poets of
real genius.

160   faults
            here
used in the sense of irregularities, exceptions to the rules of poetry. When these are justified by the poet's genius, true critics do not presume to correct them. In many editions this couplet comes after l. 151. This was Pope's first arrangement, but he later shifted it to its present position.

162   As
Kings   the
Stuart kings claimed the right to "dispense with laws," that is, to set them aside in special instances. In 1686 eleven out of twelve English judges decided in a test case that "it is a privilege inseparably connected with the sovereignty of the king to dispense with penal laws, and that according to his own judgment." The English people very naturally felt that such a privilege opened the door to absolute monarchy, and after the fall of James II, Parliament declared in 1689 that "the pretended power of suspending of laws ... without the consent of Parliament, is illegal."

164   its End
                                                             the
purpose of every law of poetry, namely, to please the reader. This
purpose must not be "transgressed," 'i.e.' forgotten by those who
wish to make exceptions to these laws.

166   their
precedent   the
example of classic poets.

179

                                                             stratage
ms ... error   things
in the classic poets which to carping critics seem faults are often
clever devices to make a deeper impression on the reader.

180   Homer
nods   Horace
in his Art of Poetry used this figure to imply that even the greatest
poet sometimes made mistakes. Pope very neatly suggests that it
may be the critic rather than the poet who is asleep.

181   each
ancient Altar   used
here to denote the works of the great classic writers. The whole
passage down to l. 200 is a noble outburst of enthusiasm for the
poets whom Pope had read so eagerly in early youth.

186

                                                             consenti
ng Pæans

                                                             unanim
ous hymns of praise.

194   must ...

found

        are not
destined to be discovered till some future time.

196

        Who is
"the last, the meanest of your sons"?

203

        bias

        mental
bent, or inclination.

208

        This
line is based upon physiological theories which are now obsolete.
According to these wind or air supplied the lack of blood or of
animal spirits in imperfectly constituted bodies. To such bodies
Pope compares those ill-regulated minds where a deficiency of
learning and natural ability is supplied by self-conceit.

216

        The
Pierian spring   the
spring of the Muses, who were called Pierides in Greek mythology.
It is used here as a symbol for learning, particularly for the study of
literature.

222

        the
lengths behind   the
great spaces of learning that lie behind the first objects of our
study.

225-232

        This
fine simile is one of the best expressions in English verse of the
modesty of the true scholar, due to his realization of the boundless
extent of knowledge. It was such a feeling that led Sir Isaac
Newton to say after all his wonderful discoveries,

"I do not know what I may appear to the world, but to myself I seem to have been only like a boy playing on the seashore and diverting myself in now and then finding a smoother pebble or a prettier shell than ordinary whilst the great ocean of truth lay all the time undiscovered before me."

224   peculiar
parts

                                                                 individu
al parts.

248   ev'n
thine, O Rome   there
are so many splendid churches in Rome that an inhabitant of this
city would be less inclined than a stranger to wonder at the perfect
proportions of any of them. But there are two, at least, the
Pantheon and St. Peter's, which might justly evoke the admiration
even of a Roman. It was probably of one of these that Pope was
thinking.

265

                                                             What is
the difference between "principles" and "notions" in this line?

265   La
Mancha's Knight   Don
Quixote. The anecdote that follows is not taken from Cervantes'
novel, but from a continuation of it by an author calling himself
Avellanada. The story is that Don Quixote once fell in with a
scholar who had written a play about a persecuted queen of
Bohemia. Her innocence in the original story was established by a
combat in the lists, but this the poet proposed to omit as contrary to
the rules of Aristotle. The Don, although professing great respect

for Aristotle, insisted that the combat was the best part of the story and must be acted, even if a special theater had to be built for the purpose, or the play given in the open fields. Pope quotes this anecdote to show how some critics in spite of their professed acceptance of general rules are so prejudiced in favor of a minor point as to judge a whole work of art from one standpoint only.

270   Dennis
John
Dennis, a playwright and critic of Pope's time. Pope and he were engaged in frequent quarrels, but this first reference to him in Pope's works is distinctly complimentary. The line probably refers to some remarks by Dennis on the Grecian stage in his Impartial Critic, a pamphlet published in 1693.

273   nice
discrimi
nating; in l. 286 the meaning is "over-scrupulous, finicky."

276   unities
accordi
ng to the laws of dramatic composition generally accepted in Pope's day, a play must observe the unities of subject, place, and time. That is, it must have one main theme, not a number of diverse stories, for its plot; all the scenes must be laid in one place, or as nearly so as possible; and the action must be begun and finished within the space of twenty-four hours.

286   curious
fastidio
us, over-particular.

288   by a
love to parts   by too
diligent attention to particular parts of a work of art, which hinders

them from forming a true judgment of the work as a whole.

289   conceit
an
uncommon or fantastic expression of thought. "Conceits" had been much sought after by the poets who wrote in the first half of the seventeenth century.

297   True
Wit   here
opposed to the "conceit" of which Pope has been speaking. It is defined as a natural idea expressed in fit words.

299   whose
truth ... find   of
whose truth we find ourselves at once convinced.

308   take
upon content   take for
granted.

311-317

Show
how Pope uses the simile of the "prismatic glass" to distinguish between "false eloquence" and "true expression."

319   decent
becomi
ng

328

Fungos
o   a
character in Ben Jonson's Every Man out of his Humour. He is the son of a miserly farmer, and tries hard, though all in vain, to imitate the dress and manners of a fine gentleman.

329

sparks   These these

would-be dandies.

337

         Number

s   rhythm,

meter.

341   haunt

Parnassus   read

poetry. — ear:' note that in Pope's day this word rhymed with "repair" and "there."

344   these

         critics

who care for the meter only in poetry insist on the proper number of syllables in a line, no matter what sort of sound or sense results. For instance, they do not object to a series of "open vowels," i. e. hiatuses caused by the juxtaposition of such words as "tho" and "oft," "the" and "ear." Line 345 is composed especially to show how feeble a rhythm results from such a succession of "open vowels." They do not object to bolstering up a line with "expletives," such as "do" in l. 346, nor to using ten "low words," i.e. short, monosyllabic words to make up a line.

347

         With

this line Pope passes unconsciously from speaking of bad critics to denouncing some of the errors of bad poets, who keep on using hackneyed phrases and worn-out metrical devices.

356

         Alexan

drine   a line of

six iambic feet, such as l. 357, written especially to illustrate this
form. Why does Pope use the adjective "needless" here?

361

Denha
m's strength ... Waller's sweetness
Waller
and Denham were poets of the century before Pope; they are
almost forgotten to-day, but were extravagantly admired in his
time. Waller began and Denham continued the fashion of writing
in "closed" heroic couplets, i.e. in verses where the sense is for the
most part contained within one couplet and does not run over into
the next as had been the fashion in earlier verse. Dryden said that
"the excellence and dignity of rhyme were never fully known till
Mr. Waller taught it," and the same critic spoke of Denham's
poetry as "majestic and correct."

370

Ajax
one of
the heroes of the Iliad. He is represented more than once as hurling
huge stones at his enemies. Note that Pope has endeavored in this
and the following line to convey the sense of effort and struggle.
What means does he employ? Do you think he succeeds?

372

Camilla
a
heroine who appears in the latter part of the Æneid fighting against
the Trojan invaders of Italy. Virgil says that she was so swift of
foot that she might have run over a field of wheat without breaking
the stalks, or across the sea without wetting her feet. Pope attempts
in l. 373 to reproduce in the sound and movement of his verse the
sense of swift flight.

374

Timoth
eus
a Greek

poet and singer who was said to have played and sung before
Alexander the Great. The reference in this passage is to Dryden's
famous poem, Alexander's Feast.

376   the son
of Libyan Jove

Alexan
der the Great, who boasted that he was the son of Jupiter. The
famous oracle of Jupiter Ammon situated in the Libyan desert was
visited by Alexander, who was said to have learned there the secret
of his parentage.

383   Dryden
                                                       this fine
compliment is paid to a poet whom Pope was proud to
acknowledge as his master. "I learned versification wholly from
Dryden's works," he once said. Pope's admiration for Dryden dated
from early youth, and while still a boy he induced a friend to take
him to see the old poet in his favorite coffee-house.

391   admire
                                                       not used
in our modern sense, but in its original meaning, "to wonder at."
According to Pope, it is only fools who are lost in wonder at the
beauties of a poem; wise men "approve," i.e. test and pronounce
them good.

396-7

Pope
acknowledged that in these lines he was alluding to the
uncharitable belief of his fellow-Catholics that all outside the fold
of the Catholic church were sure to be damned.

400

sublime

s   purifies

404   each
                                                                 each

age.

415   joins
with Quality   takes
sides with "the quality," i.e. people of rank.

429   Are
so clever that they refuse to accept the common and true belief,
and so forfeit their salvation.

441

                                                                 sentenc
es   the
reference is to a mediaeval treatise on Theology, by Peter
Lombard, called the Book of Sentences. It was long used as a
university text-book.

444   Scotists
and Thomists

                                                                 mediæv
al scholars, followers respectively of Duns Scotus and Thomas
Aquinas. A long dispute raged between their disciples. In this
couplet Pope points out that the dispute is now forgotten, and the
books of the old disputants lie covered with cobwebs in Duck-lane,
a street in London where second-hand books were sold in Pope's
day. He calls the cobwebs "kindred," because the arguments of
Thomists and Scotists were as fine spun as a spider's web.

449

                                                                 "The
latest fashionable folly is the test, or the proof, of a quick, up-to-

date wit." In other words, to be generally accepted an author must accept the current fashion, foolish though it may be.

457   This was especially true in Pope's day when literature was so closely connected with politics that an author's work was praised or blamed not upon its merits, but according to his, and the critic's, politics.

459   Parsons, Critics, Beaus   Dryden, the head of English letters in the generation before Pope, had been bitterly assailed on various charges by parsons, like Jeremy Collier, critics like Milbourn, and fine gentlemen like the Duke of Buckingham. But his works remained when the jests that were made against them were forgotten.

463   Sir Richard Blackmore, a famous doctor in Dryden's day, was also a very dull and voluminous writer. He attacked Dryden in a poem called A Satire against Wit. Luke Milbourn was a clergyman of the same period, who abused Dryden's translation of Virgil.

465   Zoilus
          a Greek

critic who attacked Homer.

481   The English language and the public taste had changed very rapidly during the century preceding Pope. He imagined that these changes would continue so that no poet's reputation would last longer than a man's life, "bare threescore," and Dryden's poetry would come to be as hard to understand and as little read as Chaucer's at that time. It is worth noting that both Dryden and Pope rewrote parts of

Chaucer in modern English.

506-7

Explain why "wit" is feared by wicked men and shunned by the virtuous, hated by fools, and "undone" or ruined by knaves.

521 sacred accurse

d, like the Latin sacer.

527 spleen bad

temper.

534 the fat age the

reign of Charles II, as ll. 536-537 show, when literature became notoriously licentious.

538 Jilts ... statesmen loose

women like Lady Castlemaine and the Duchess of Portsmouth had great influence on the politics of Charles II's time, and statesmen of that day like Buckingham and Etheredge wrote comedies.

541 mask it was

not uncommon in Restoration times for ladies to wear a mask in public, especially at the theater. Here the word is used to denote the woman who wore a mask.

544 a Foreign reign the

reign of William III, a Dutchman. Pope, as a Tory and a Catholic, hated the memory of William, and here asserts, rather unfairly, that his age was marked by an increase of heresy and infidelity.

545   Socinus
             the
name of two famous heretics, uncle and nephew, of the sixteenth
century, who denied the divinity of Christ.

549

             Pope
insinuates here that the clergy under William III hated an absolute
monarch so much that they even encouraged their hearers to
question the absolute power of God.

551   admir'd
           see note

to l. 391.

552   Wit's
Titans   wits
who defied heaven as the old Titans did the gods. The reference is
to a group of freethinkers who came into prominence in King
William's reign.

556

           scandal
ously nice   so over-
particular as to find cause for scandal where none exists.

557   mistake
an author into vice

           mistake
nly read into an author vicious ideas which are not really to be
found in his work.

575

           Things

that men really do not know must be brought forward modestly as if they had only been forgotten for a time.

577   that
only   good-
breeding alone

585   Appius
                                         a
nickname for John Dennis, taken from his tragedy, Appius and Virginia, which appeared two years before the Essay on Criticism. Lines 585-587 hit off some of the personal characteristics of this hot-tempered critic. "Tremendous" was a favorite word with Dennis.

588   tax
                                      blame,

find fault with.

591   In
Pope's time noblemen could take degrees at the English universities without passing the regular examinations.

617

                                     Dryden's Fables published in 1700 represented the very best narrative poetry of the greatest poet of his day. D'Urfey's Tales, on the other hand, published in 1704 and 1706, were collections of dull and obscene doggerel by a wretched poet.

618   with
him

                                     according to "the bookful blockhead."

619   Garth

a well-known doctor of the day, who wrote a much admired mock-heroic poem called The Dispensary. His enemies asserted that he was not really the author of the poem.

623

Such foolish critics are just as ready to pour out their opinions on a man in St. Paul's cathedral as in the bookseller's shops in the square around the church, which is called St. Paul's churchyard.

632   proud to
know   proud
of his knowledge.

636

                                humanl
y   an old
form for "humanely."

642   love to
praise   a love
of praising men.

648

                                Mæonia
n Star   Homer.
Mæonia, or Lydia, was a district in Asia which was said to have been the birthplace of Homer.

652

                                conquer
ed Nature

                                Aristotl
e was a master of all the knowledge of nature extant in his day.

653   Horace the

famous Latin poet whose Ars Poetica was one of Pope's models for the Essay on Criticism.

662   fle'me phlegm,

according to old ideas of physiology, one of the four "humours" or fluids which composed the body. Where it abounded it made men dull and heavy, or as we still say "phlegmatic."

663-4   A

rather confused couplet. It means, "Horace suffers as much by the misquotations critics make from his work as by the bad translations that wits make of them."

665

                                               Dionysius

                                               Dionysius

us of Halicarnassus, a famous Greek critic. Pope's manner of reference to him seems to show that he had never read his works.

667

                                               Petronia

courtier and man of letters of the time of Nero. Only a few lines of his remaining work contain any criticism.

669

                                             Quintilian's work the

Institutiones Oratoriæ of Quintilianus, a famous Latin critic of the first century A.D.

675 Longinus a Greek critic of the third century A.D., who composed a famous work called A Treatise on the Sublime. It is a work showing high imagination as well as careful reasoning, and hence Pope speaks of the author as inspired by the Nine, i. e. the Muses.

692 The willful hatred of the monks for the works of classical antiquity tended to complete that destruction of old books which the Goths began when they sacked the Roman cities. Many ancient writings were erased, for example, in order to get parchment for monkish chronicles and commentaries.

693 Erasmus perhaps the greatest scholar of the Renaissance. Pope calls him the "glory of the priesthood" on account of his being a monk of such extraordinary learning, and "the shame" of his order, because he was so abused by monks in his lifetime. Is this a good antithesis?

697 Leo's golden days the pontificate of Leo X (1513-1521). Leo himself was a generous patron of art and learning. He paid particular attention to sacred music (1. 703), and engaged Raphael to decorate the Vatican with frescoes. Vida (1. 704) was an Italian poet of his time, who became famous by the excellence of his Latin verse. One of his poems was on the art of poetry, and it is to this that Pope refers in l. 706.

707-8 Cremona was the birthplace of Vida; Mantua, of Virgil.

709   The

allusion is to the sack of Rome by the Constable Bourbon's army in 1527. This marked the end of the golden age of arts in Italy.

714   Boileau

a

French poet and critic (1636-1711). His L'Art Poetique is founded on Horace's Ars Poetica.

723   the

Muse   i. e. the

genius, of John Sheffield (1649-1720), Duke of Buckingham (not to be confounded with Dryden's enemy). Line 724 is quoted from his Essay on Poetry.

725

                                                      Roscom

mon

                                                      Wentw

orth Dillon (1633-1684), Earl of Roscommon, author of a translation of the Ars Poetica and of An Essay on Translated Verse.

729   Walsh

a

commonplace poet (1663-1708), but apparently a good critic. Dryden, in fact, called him the best critic in the nation. He was an early friend and judicious adviser of Pope himself, who showed him much of his early work, including the first draft of this very poem. Pope was sincerely attached to him, and this tribute to his dead friend is marked by deep and genuine feeling.

738   short

excursions   such as

this Essay on Criticism instead of longer and more ambitious poems which Pope planned and in part executed in his boyhood. There is no reason to believe with Mr. Elwin that this passage proves that Pope formed the design of the poem after the death of Walsh.

Contents

Notes on An Essay on Man, Epistle I

Introduction

The Essay on Man is the longest and in some ways the most important work of the third period of Pope's career. It corresponds closely to his early work, the Essay on Criticism. Like the earlier work, the Essay on Man is a didactic poem, written primarily to diffuse and popularize certain ideas of the poet. As in the earlier work these ideas are by no means original with Pope, but were the common property of a school of thinkers in his day. As in the Essay on Criticism, Pope here attempts to show that these ideas have their origin in nature and are consistent with the common sense of man. And finally the merit of the later work, even more than of the earlier, is due to the force and brilliancy of detached passages rather than to any coherent, consistent, and well-balanced system which it presents.

The close of the seventeenth century and beginning of the eighteenth was marked by a change of ground in the sphere of religious controversy. The old debates between the Catholic and Protestant churches gradually died out as these two branches of Western Christianity settled down in quiet possession of the territory they still occupy. In their place arose a vigorous controversy on the first principles of religion in general, on the nature of God, the origin of evil, the place of man in the universe, and the respective merits of optimism and pessimism as philosophic theories. The controversialists as a rule either rejected or neglected the dogmas of revealed religion and based their arguments upon real or supposed facts of history, physical nature, and the mental processes and moral characteristics of man. In this controversy the two parties at times were curiously mingled. Orthodox clergymen used arguments which justified a strong suspicion of their orthodoxy; and avowed freethinkers bitterly disclaimed the imputation of atheism and wrote in terms that might be easily adopted by a devout believer.

Into this controversy Pope was led by his deepening intimacy with Bolingbroke, who had returned from France in 1725 and settled at his country place within a few miles of Twickenham. During his long exile Bolingbroke had amused himself with the study of moral philosophy and natural religion, and in his frequent intercourse with Pope he poured out his new-found opinions with all the fluency, vigor, and polish which made him so famous among the orators and talkers of the day. Bolingbroke's views were for that time distinctly heterodox, and, if logically developed, led to complete agnosticism. But he seems to have avoided a complete statement of his ideas to Pope, possibly for fear of shocking or frightening the sensitive little poet who still remained a professed Catholic. Pope, however, was very far from being a strict Catholic, and indeed prided himself on the breadth and liberality of his opinions. He was, therefore, at once fascinated and stimulated by the eloquent conversation of Bolingbroke, and resolved to write a philosophical poem in which to embody the ideas they held in common. Bolingbroke approved of the idea, and went so far as to furnish the poet with seven or eight sheets of notes "to direct the plan in general and to supply matter for particular epistles." Lord Bathurst, who knew both Pope and Bolingbroke, went so far as to say in later years that the Essay was originally composed by Bolingbroke in prose and that Pope only put it into verse. But this is undoubtedly an exaggeration of what Pope himself frankly acknowledged, that the poem was composed under the influence of Bolingbroke, that in the main it reflected his opinions, and that Bolingbroke had assisted him in the general plan and in numerous details. Very properly, therefore, the poem is addressed to Bolingbroke and begins and closes with a direct address to the poet's "guide, philosopher, and friend."

In substance the Essay on Man is a discussion of the moral order of the world. Its purpose is "to vindicate the ways of God to man," and it may therefore be regarded as an attempt to confute the skeptics who argued from the existence of evil in the world and the wretchedness of man's existence to the impossibility of belief in an all-good and all-wise God. It attempts to do this, not by an appeal to revelation or the doctrines of Christianity, but simply on the basis of a common-sense interpretation of the facts of existence.

A brief outline of the poem will show the general tenor of Pope's argument.

The first epistle deals with the nature and state of man with respect to the universe. It insists on the limitations of man's knowledge, and the consequent absurdity of his presuming to murmur against God. It teaches that the universe was not made for man, but that man with all his apparent imperfections is exactly fitted to the place which he occupies in the universe. In the physical universe all things work together for good, although certain aspects of nature seem evil to man, and likewise in the moral universe all things, even man's passions and crimes conduce to the general good of the whole. Finally it urges calm submission and acquiescence in what is hard to understand, since "one truth is clear, — whatever is, is right."

The second epistle deals with the nature of man as an individual. It begins by urging men to abandon vain questionings of God's providence and to take up the consideration of their own natures, for "the proper study of mankind is man." Pope points out that the two cardinal principles of man's nature are self-love and reason, the first an impelling, the second a regulating power. The aim of both these principles is pleasure, by which Pope means happiness, which he takes for the highest good. Each man is dominated by a master passion, and it is the proper function of reason to control this passion for good and to make it bear fruit in virtue. No man is wholly virtuous or vicious, and Heaven uses the mingled qualities of men to bind them together in mutual interdependence, and makes the various passions and imperfections of mankind serve the general good. And the final conclusion is that "though man's a fool, yet God is wise."

The third epistle treats of the nature of man with respect to society. All creatures, Pope asserts, are bound together and live not for themselves alone, but man is preeminently a social being. The first state of man was the state of nature when he lived in innocent ignorance with his fellow-creatures. Obeying the voice of nature, man learned to copy and improve upon the instincts of the animals, to build, to plow, to spin, to unite in societies like those of ants and bees. The first form of government was patriarchal; then monarchies arose in which virtue, "in arms or arts," made one man ruler over many. In either case the origin of true government as of true religion was love. Gradually force crept in and uniting with superstition gave rise to tyranny and false religions. Poets and patriots, however, restored the ancient faith and taught power's due use by showing the necessity of harmony in the state. Pope concludes by asserting the folly of contention for forms of government or modes of faith. The common end of government as of religion is the general good. It may be noticed in passing that Pope's account of the evolution of society bears even less relation to historical facts than does his account of the development of literature in the Essay on Criticism.

The last epistle discusses the nature of happiness, "our being's end and aim." Happiness is attainable by all men who think right and mean well. It consists not in individual, but in mutual pleasure. It does not consist in external things, mere gifts of fortune, but in health, peace, and competence. Virtuous men are, indeed, subject to calamities of nature; but God cannot be expected to suspend the operation of general laws to spare the virtuous. Objectors who would construct a system in which all virtuous men are blest, are challenged to define the virtuous and to specify what is meant by blessings. Honors, nobility, fame, superior talents, often merely serve to make their possessors unhappy. Virtue alone is happiness, and virtue consists in a recognition of the laws of Providence, and in love for one's fellow-man.

Even this brief outline will show, I think, some of the inconsistencies and omissions of Pope's train of thought. A careful examination of his arguments in detail would be wholly out of place here. The reader who wishes to pursue the subject further may consult Warburton's elaborate vindication of Pope's argument, and Elwin's equally prosy refutation, or better still the admirable summary by Leslie Stephen in the chapter on this poem in his life of Pope (English Men of Letters). No one is now likely to turn to the writer of the early eighteenth century for a system of the universe, least of all to a writer so incapable of exact or systematic thinking as Alexander Pope. If the Essay on Man has any claim to be read to-day, it must be as a piece of literature pure and simple. For philosophy and poetry combined, Browning and Tennyson lie nearer to our age and mode of thought than Pope.

Even regarded as a piece of literature the Essay on Man cannot, I think, claim the highest place among Pope's works. It obtained, indeed, a success at home and abroad such as was achieved by no other English poem until the appearance of Childe Harold. It was translated into French, German, Italian, Portuguese, Polish, and Latin. It was imitated by Wieland, praised by Voltaire, and quoted by Kant. But this success was due in part to the accuracy with which it reflected ideas which were the common property of its age, in part to the extraordinary vigor and finish of its epigrams, which made it one of the most quotable of English poems. But as a whole the Essay is not a great poem. The poet is evidently struggling with a subject that is too weighty for him, and at times he staggers and sinks beneath his burden. The second and third books in particular are, it must be confessed, with the exception of one or two fine outbursts, little better than dull, and dullness is not a quality one is accustomed to associate with Pope. The Essay on Man lacks the bright humor and imaginative artistry of The Rape of the Lock, and the lively portraiture, vigorous satire, and strong personal note of the Moral Epistles and Imitations of Horace. Pope is at his best when he is dealing with a concrete world of men and women as they lived and moved in the London of his day; he is at his worst when he is attempting to seize and render abstract ideas.

Yet the Essay on Man is a very remarkable work. In the first place, it shows Pope's wonderful power of expression. No one can read the poem for the first time without meeting on page after page phrases and epigrams which have become part of the common currency of our language. Pope's "precision and firmness of touch," to quote the apt statement of Leslie Stephen, "enables him to get the greatest possible meaning into a narrow compass. He uses only one epithet, but it is the right one." Even when the thought is commonplace enough, the felicity of the expression gives it a new and effective force. And there are whole passages where Pope rises high above the mere coining of epigrams. As I have tried to show in my notes he composed by separate paragraphs, and when he chances upon a topic that appeals to his imagination or touches his heart, we get an outburst of poetry that shines in splendid contrast to the prosaic plainness of its surroundings. Such, for example, are the noble verses that tell of the immanence of God in his creation at the close of the first epistle, or the magnificent invective against tyranny and superstition in the third (ll. 241-268).

Finally the Essay on Man is of interest in what it tells us of Pope himself. Mr. Elwin's idea that in the Essay on Man Pope, "partly the dupe, partly the accomplice of Bolingbroke," was attempting craftily to undermine the foundations of religion, is a notion curiously compounded of critical blindness and theological rancor. In spite of all its incoherencies and futilities the Essay is an honest attempt to express Pope's opinions, borrowed in part, of course, from his admired friend, but in part the current notions of his age, on some of the greatest questions that have perplexed the mind of man. And Pope's attitude toward the questions is that of the best minds of his day, at once religious, independent, and sincere. He acknowledges the omnipotence and benevolence of God, confesses the limitations and imperfections of human knowledge, teaches humility in the presence of unanswerable problems, urges submission to Divine Providence, extols virtue as the true source of happiness, and love of man as an essential of virtue. If we study the Essay on Man as the reasoned argument of a philosopher, we shall turn from it with something like contempt; if we read it as the expression of a poet's sentiments, we shall, I think, leave it with an admiration warmer than before for a character that has been so much abused and so little understood as that of Pope.

line

referenc

e

meanin

g

The Design

2   Bacon's
expression   in the
dedication of his Essays (1625) to Buckingham, Bacon speaks of
them as the most popular of his writings, "for that, as it seems, they
come home to men's business and bosoms."

11
                                                                   anatom
y
                                                                   dissecti
on

Epistle I

1   St. John
                                                                   Henry
St. John, Lord Bolingbroke, Pope's "guide, philosopher, and
friend," under whose influence the Essay on Man was composed.

5
                                                                   expatiat
e   range,
wander.

6
                                                                   Pope
says that this line alludes to the subject of this first Epistle, "the
state of man here and hereafter, disposed by Providence, though to
him unknown." The next two lines allude to the main topics of the
three remaining epistles, "the constitution of the human mind ... the
temptations of misapplied self-love, and the wrong pursuits of
power, pleasure, and false happiness."

9   beat ...
field   the
metaphor is drawn from hunting. Note how it is elaborated in the
following lines.

12   blindly
creep ... sightless soar   the first
are the ignorant and indifferent; those who "sightless soar" are the
presumptuous who reason blindly about things too high for human
knowledge.

15   candid
           lenient,
free from harsh judgments.

16   An
adaptation of a well-known line of Milton's Paradise Lost, l, 26.

17-23

           Pope
lays down as the basis of his system that all argument about man or
God must be based upon what we know of man's present life, and
of God's workings in this world of ours.

29   this
frame   the
universe. Compare Hamlet, II, ii, 310, "this goodly frame, the
earth."

30   nice
dependencies   subtle
inter-relations.

31

           Gradati
ons just   exact

shades of difference.

32   a part
the

mind of man, which is but a part of the whole universe.

33   the
great chain

accordi

ng to Homer, Jove, the supreme God, sustained the whole creation by a golden chain. Milton also makes use of this idea of the visible universe as linked to heaven in a golden chain, Paradise Lost, II, 1004-1006, and 1051-1052.

41   yonder
argent fields   the sky
spangled with silvery stars. The phrase is borrowed from Milton, Paradise Lost, III, 460.

42   Jove
the

planet Jupiter.

satellite
s   Pope
preserves here the Latin pronunciation, four syllables, with the accent on the antepenult.

43-40

Pope

here takes it for granted that our universe, inasmuch as it is the work of God's infinite wisdom, must be the best system possible. If this be granted, he says, it is plain that man must have a place somewhere in this system, and the only question is whether "God has placed him wrong."

45

Every grade in creation must be complete, so as to join with that which is beneath and with that which is above it or there would be a lack of coherency, a break, somewhere in the system.

47

reas'nin g life

conscio us mental life.

51-60

Pope argues here that since man is a part of the best possible system, whatever seems wrong in him must be right when considered in relation to the whole order of the universe. It is only our ignorance of this order which keeps us from realizing this fact.

55   one
single   the
word "movement" is understood after "single."

61-8

Pope here illustrates his preceding argument by analogy. We can know no more of God's purpose in the ordering of our lives than the animals can know of our ordering of theirs.

64   Ægypt's
God   One of
the gods of the Egyptians was the sacred bull, Apis.

68   a deity
         worship

ed as a god, like the Egyptian kings and Roman emperors.

69-76

Pope now goes on to argue that on the basis of what has been proved we ought not to regard man as an imperfect being, but rather as one who is perfectly adapted to his place in the universe. His knowledge, for example, is measured by the brief time he has to live and the brief space he can survey.

69

fault

pronoun ced in Pope's day as rhyming with "ought."

73-6

These lines are really out of place. They first appeared after l. 98; then Pope struck them out altogether. Just before his death he put them into their present place on the advice of Warburton, who probably approved of them because of their reference to a future state of bliss. It is plain that they interfere with the regular argument of the poem.

79

This line is grammatically dependent upon "hides," l. 77.

81

riot

used here in the sense of "luxurious life." The lamb is slain to provide for some feast.

86

Heav'n

i. e. God. Hence the relative "who" in the next line.

92-8

Pope urges man to comfort himself with hope, seeing that he cannot know the future.

93 What the future bliss words "shall be" are to be understood after this phrase.

96

Point out the exact meaning of this familiar line.

97 from home away from its true home, the life to come. This line represents one of the alterations which Warburton induced Pope to make. The poet first wrote "confined at home," thus representing this life as the home of the soul. His friend led him to make the change in order to express more clearly his belief in the soul's immortality.

89

Show how "rests" and "expatiates" in this line contrast with "uneasy" and "confined" in l. 97.

99-112 In this famous passage Pope shows how the belief in immortality is found even among the most ignorant tribes. This is to Pope an argument that the soul must be immortal, since only Nature, or God working through Nature, could have implanted this conception in the Indian's mind.

102 the the solar walk sun's path in the heavens.

the

milky way   some

old philosophers held that the souls of good men went thither after
death.

...

Pope

means that the ignorant Indian had no conception of a heaven
reserved for the just such as Greek sages and Christian believers
have. All he believes in is "an humbler heaven," where he shall be
free from the evils of this life. Line 108 has special reference to the
tortures inflicted upon the natives of Mexico and Peru by the
avaricious Spanish conquerors.

109-10   He

is contented with a future existence, without asking for the glories
of the Christian's heaven.

111   equal

sky

impartia

l heaven, for the heaven of the Indians was open to all men, good
or bad.

113-30   In

this passage Pope blames those civilized men who, though they
should be wiser than the Indian, murmur against the decrees of
God. The imperative verbs "weigh," "call," "say," etc., are used
satirically.

113   scale of

sense   the

scale, or means of judgment, which our senses give us.

117   gust

the

pleasure of taste.

120   The
murmurers are dissatisfied that man is not at once perfect in his
present state and destined to immortality, although such gifts have
been given to no other creature.

123

reas'nin
g pride   the
pride of the intellect which assumes to condemn God's providence.

131-172   In
this passage Pope imagines a dialogue between one of the proud
murmurers he has described and himself. His opponent insists that
the world was made primarily for man's enjoyment (ll. 132-140).
Pope asks whether nature does not seem to swerve from this end of
promoting human happiness in times of pestilence, earthquake, and
tempest (ll. 141-144). The other answers that these are only rare
exceptions to the general laws, due perhaps to some change in
nature since the world began (ll. 145-148). Pope replies by asking
why there should not be exceptions in the moral as well as in the
physical world; may not great villains be compared to terrible
catastrophes in nature (ll. 148-156)? He goes on to say that no one
but God can answer this question, that our human reasoning
springs from pride, and that the true course of reasoning is simply
to submit (ll. 156-164). He then suggests that "passions," by which
he means vices, are as necessary a part of the moral order as storms
of the physical world (ll. 165-172).

142   livid
deaths

pestilen
ce

143-4

Pope was perhaps thinking of a terrible earthquake and flood that had caused great loss of life in Chili the year before this poem appeared.

150   then
Nature deviates   Nature departs from her regular order on such occasions as these catastrophes.

151   that end human happiness, as in l. 149.

156

Cæsar Borgia, the wicked son of Pope Alexander VI, and Catiline are mentioned here as portents in the moral world parallel to plagues and earthquakes in the physical.

160   young
Ammon

Alexan der the Great. See note on Essay on Criticism, l. 376.

163

Why do we accuse God for permitting wickedness when we do not blame Him for permitting evil in the natural world?

166   there
in nature

here

in man

173-206 In this section Pope reproves those who are dissatisfied with man's faculties. He points out that all animals, man included, have powers suited to their position in the world (ll. 179-188), and asserts that if man had keener senses than he now has, he would be exposed to evils from which he now is free (ll. 193-203).

176 to want to lack

177 Paraphrase this line in prose.

181 compensated accented on the antepenult.

183 the state the place which the creature occupies in the natural world.

195 finer keener optics power of sight.

197 touch a noun, subject of "were given," understood from l. 195.

199 quick pungent effluvia

odors. The construction is very condensed here; "effluvia" may be regarded like "touch" as a subject of "were given" (l. 195); but one would expect rather a phrase to denote a keener sense of smell than man now possesses.

202   music
of the spheres   it was
an old belief that the stars and planets uttered musical notes as they moved along their courses. These notes made up the "harmony of the spheres." Shakespeare ('Merchant of Venice', V, 64-5) says that our senses are too dull to hear it. Pope, following a passage in Cicero's Somnium Scipionis, suggests that this music is too loud for human senses.

207-232
                                                                            Pope
now goes on to show how in the animal world there is an exact gradation of the faculties of sense and of the powers of instinct. Man alone is endowed with reason which is more than equivalent to all these powers and makes him lord over all animals.

212   The
mole is almost blind; the lynx was supposed to be the most keen-sighted of animals.

213-4   The
lion was supposed by Pope to hunt by sight alone as the dog by scent. What does he mean by "the tainted green"?

215-6
                                                                            Fishes
are almost deaf, while birds are very quick of hearing.

219   nice
                                                                            keenly

discriminating.

healing

dew

healthfu

l honey.

221-222   The
power of instinct which is barely perceptible in the pig amounts
almost to the power of reason in the elephant.

223   barrier

pronoun

ced like the French 'barrière', as a word of two syllables with the
accent on the last.

226   Sense ...
Thought

sensatio

n and reason.

227   middle
natures

interme

diate natures, which long to unite with those above or below them.
The exact sense is not very clear.

233-58   In
this passage Pope insists that the chain of being stretches unbroken
from God through man to the lowest created forms. If any link in
this chain were broken, as would happen if men possessed higher
faculties than are now assigned them, the whole universe would be
thrown into confusion. This is another answer to those who
complain of the imperfections of man's nature.

234   quick

living.
Pope does not discriminate between organic and inorganic matter.

240   glass

microsc
ope

242-44

Inferior
beings might then press upon us. If they did not, a fatal gap would
be left by our ascent in the scale.

247   each
system   Pope
imagines the universe to be composed of an infinite number of
systems like ours. Since each of these is essential to the orderly
arrangement of the universe, any disorder such as he has imagined
would have infinitely destructive consequences. These are
described in ll. 251-257.

267-80   In
these lines Pope speaks of God as the soul of the world in an
outburst of really exalted enthusiasm that is rare enough in his
work.

269   thata
relative pronoun referring to "soul," l. 268.

270   th'
ethereal frame   the
heavens

276   as
perfect in a hair as heart   this has
been called "a vile antithesis," on the ground that there is no reason
why hair and heart should be contrasted. But Pope may have had in

mind the saying of Christ. "the very hairs of your head are all numbered." The hairs are spoken of here as the least important part of the body; the heart, on the other hand, has always been thought of as the most important organ. There is, therefore, a real antithesis between the two.

278   Seraph
... burns   the
seraphim according to old commentators are on fire with the love of God.

280   equals
all   makes
all things equal. This does not seem consistent with the idea of the gradations of existence which Pope has been preaching throughout this Epistle. Possibly it means that all things high and low are filled alike with the divine spirit and in this sense all things are equal. But one must not expect to find exact and consistent philosophy in the Essay on Man.

281-94

                                                                             Here
Pope sums up the argument of this Epistle, urging man to recognize his ignorance, to be content with his seeming imperfections, and to realize that "whatever is, is right."

282   our
proper bliss   our
happiness as men.

283   point
                                                                             appoint
ed place in the universe.

286   Secure

sure.

289

Hobbes, an English philosopher with whose work Pope was, no doubt, acquainted, says, "Nature is the art whereby God governs the world."

Contents

An Epistle to Dr. Arbuthnot

Introduction

Next to The Rape of the Lock, I think, the Epistle to Arbuthnot is the most interesting and the most important of Pope's poems — the most important since it shows the master poet of the age employing his ripened powers in the field most suitable for their display, that of personal satire, the most interesting, because, unlike his former satiric poem the Dunciad, it is not mere invective, but gives us, as no other poem of Pope's can be said to do, a portrait of the poet himself.

Like most of Pope's poems, the Epistle to Arbuthnot owes its existence to an objective cause. This was the poet's wish to justify himself against a series of savage attacks, which had recently been directed against him. If Pope had expected by the publication of the Dunciad to crush the herd of scribblers who had been for years abusing him, he must have been woefully disappointed. On the contrary, the roar of insult and calumny rose louder than ever, and new voices were added to the chorus. In the year 1733 two enemies entered the field against Pope such as he had never yet had to encounter — enemies of high social position, of acknowledged wit, and of a certain, though as the sequel proved quite inadequate, talent for satire. These were Lady Mary Wortley Montague and Lord John Hervey.

Lady Mary had been for years acknowledged as one of the wittiest, most learned, and most beautiful women of her day. Pope seems to have met her in 1715 and at once joined the train of her admirers. When she accompanied her husband on his embassy to Constantinople in the following year, the poet entered into a long correspondence with her, protesting in the most elaborate fashion his undying devotion. On her return he induced her to settle with her husband at Twickenham. Here he continued his attentions, half real, half in the affected gallantry of the day, until, to quote the lady's own words to her daughter many years after,

"at some ill-chosen time when she least expected what romancers call a declaration, he made such passionate love to her, as, in spite of her utmost endeavours to be angry and look grave, provoked an immoderate fit of laughter," and, she added, from that moment Pope became her implacable enemy. Certainly by the time Pope began to write the Dunciad he was so far estranged from his old friend that he permitted himself in that poem a scoffing allusion to a scandal in which she had recently become involved. The lady answered, or the poet thought that she did, with an anonymous pamphlet, A Pop upon Pope, describing a castigation, wholly imaginary, said to have been inflicted upon the poet as a proper reward for his satire. After this, of course, all hope of a reconciliation was at an end, and in his satires and epistles Pope repeatedly introduced Lady Mary under various titles in the most offensive fashion. In his first Imitation of Horace, published in February, 1733, he referred in the most unpardonable manner to a certain Sappho, and the dangers attendant upon any acquaintance with her. Lady Mary was foolish enough to apply the lines to herself and to send a common friend to remonstrate with Pope. He coolly replied that he was surprised that Lady Mary should feel hurt, since the lines could only apply to certain women, naming four notorious scribblers, whose lives were as immoral as their works. Such an answer was by no means calculated to turn away the lady's wrath, and for an ally in the campaign of anonymous abuse that she now planned she sought out her friend Lord Hervey. John Hervey, called by courtesy Lord Hervey, the second son of the Earl of Bristol, was one of the most prominent figures at the court of George II. He had been made vice-chamberlain of the royal household in 1730, and was the intimate friend and confidential adviser of Queen Caroline. Clever, affable, unprincipled, and cynical, he was a perfect type of the Georgian courtier to whom loyalty, patriotism, honesty, and honor were so many synonyms for folly. He was effeminate in habits and appearance, but notoriously licentious; he affected to scoff at learning but made some pretense to literature, and had written Four Epistles after the Manner of Ovid, and numerous political pamphlets. Pope, who had some slight personal acquaintance with him, disliked his political connections and probably despised his verses, and in the Imitation already mentioned had alluded to him under the title of Lord Fanny as capable of turning out a thousand lines of verse a day. This was sufficient cause, if cause were needed, to induce Hervey to join Lady Mary in her warfare against Pope.

The first blow was struck in an anonymous poem, probably the combined work of the two allies, called Verses addressed to the Imitator of Horace, which appeared in March, 1733, and it was followed up in August by an Epistle from a Nobleman to a Doctor of Divinity, which also appeared anonymously, but was well known to be the work of Lord Hervey. In these poems Pope was abused in the most unmeasured terms. His work was styled a mere collection of libels; he had no invention except in defamation; he was a mere pretender to genius. His morals were not left unimpeached; he was charged with selling other men's work printed in his name, — a gross distortion of his employing assistants in the translation of the Odyssey, — he was ungrateful, unjust, a foe to human kind, an enemy like the devil to all that have being. The noble authors, probably well aware how they could give the most pain, proceeded to attack his family and his distorted person. His parents were obscure and vulgar people; and he himself a wretched outcast:

with the emblem of [his] crooked mind

Marked on [his] back like Cain by God's own hand.

And to cap the climax, as soon as these shameful libels were in print, Lord Hervey bustled off to show them to the Queen and to laugh with her over the fine way in which he had put down the bitter little poet.

In order to understand and appreciate Pope's reception of these attacks, we must recall to ourselves the position in which he lived. He was a Catholic, and I have already (Introduction) called attention to the precarious, tenure by which the Catholics of his time held their goods, their persons, their very lives, in security. He was the intimate of Bolingbroke, of all men living the most detested by the court, and his noble friends were almost without exception the avowed enemies of the court party. Pope had good reason to fear that the malice of his enemies might not be content to stop with abusive doggerel. But he was not in the least intimidated. On the contrary, he broke out in a fine flame of wrath against Lord Hervey, whom he evidently considered the chief offender, challenged his enemy to disavow the Epistle, and on his declining to do so, proceeded to make what he called "a proper reply" in a prose Letter to a Noble Lord. This masterly piece of satire was passed about from hand to hand, but never printed. We are told that Sir Robert Walpole, who found Hervey a convenient tool in court intrigues, bribed Pope not to print it by securing a good position in France for one of the priests who had watched over the poet's youth. If this story be true, and we have Horace Walpole's authority for it, we may well imagine that the entry of the bribe, like that of Uncle Toby's oath, was blotted out by a tear from the books of the Recording Angel.

But Pope was by no means disposed to let the attacks go without an answer of some kind, and the particular form which his answer took seems to have been suggested by a letter from Arbuthnot.

"I make it my last request," wrote his beloved physician, now sinking fast under the diseases that brought him to the grave, "that you continue that noble disdain and abhorrence of vice, which you seem so naturally endued with, but still with a due regard to your own safety; and study more to reform than to chastise, though the one often cannot be effected without the other."

"I took very kindly your advice," Pope replied, "... and it has worked so much upon me considering the time and state you gave it in, that I determined to address to you one of my epistles written by piecemeal many years, and which I have now made haste to put together; wherein the question is stated, what were, and are my motives of writing, the objections to them, and my answers."

In other words, the Epistle to Arbuthnot which we see that Pope was working over at the date of this letter, August 25, 1734, was, in the old-fashioned phrase, his Apologia, his defense of his life and work.

As usual, Pope's account of his work cannot be taken literally. A comparison of dates shows that the Epistle instead of having been "written by piecemeal many years" is essentially the work of one impulse, the desire to vindicate his character, his parents, and his work from the aspersions cast upon them by Lord Hervey and Lady Mary. The exceptions to this statement are two, or possibly three, passages which we know to have been written earlier and worked into the poem with infinite art.

The first of these is the famous portrait of Addison as Atticus. I
have already spoken of the reasons that led to Pope's breach with
Addison (Introduction); and there is good reason to believe that
this portrait sprang directly from Pope's bitter feeling toward the
elder writer for his preference of Tickell's translation. The lines
were certainly written in Addison's lifetime, though we may be
permitted to doubt whether Pope really did send them to him, as he
once asserted. They did not appear in print, however, till four years
after Addison's death, when they were printed apparently without
Pope's consent in a volume of miscellanies. It is interesting to note
that in this form the full name "Addison" appeared in the last line.
Some time later Pope acknowledged the verses and printed them
with a few changes in his Miscellany of 1727, substituting the
more decorous "A — -n" for the "Addison" of the first text. Finally
he worked over the passage again and inserted it, for a purpose that
will be shown later, in the Epistle to Arbuthnot.

It is not worth while to discuss here the justice or injustice of this
famous portrait. In fact, the question hardly deserves to be raised.
The passage is admittedly a satire, and a satire makes no claim to
be a just and final sentence. Admitting, as we must, that Pope was
in the wrong in his quarrel with Addison, we may well admit that
he has not done him full justice. But we must equally admit that
the picture is drawn with wonderful skill, that praise and blame are
deftly mingled, and that the satire is all the more severe because of
its frank admission of the great man's merits. And it must also be
said that Pope has hit off some of the faults of Addison's character,
— his coldness, his self-complacency, his quiet sneer, his
indulgence of flattering fools — in a way that none of his
biographers have done. That Pope was not blind to Addison's chief

merit as an author is fully shown by a passage in a later poem, less well known than the portrait of Atticus, but well worth quotation. After speaking of the licentiousness of literature in Restoration days, he goes on to say:

In our own (excuse some courtly stains)

No whiter page than Addison's remains,

He from the taste obscene reclaims our youth,

And sets the passions on the side of truth,

Forms the soft bosom with the gentlest art,

And pours each human virtue in the heart.

Epistle to Augustus, II. 215-220.

If Pope was unjust to Addison the man, he at least made amends to Addison the moralist.

The second passage that may have had an independent existence before the Epistle was conceived is the portrait of Bufo, ll. 229-247. There is reason to believe that this attack was first aimed at Bubb Doddington, a courtier of Hervey's class, though hardly of so finished a type, to whom Pope alludes as Bubo in l. 278. When Pope was working on the Epistle, however, he saw an opportunity to vindicate his own independence of patronage by a satiric portrait of the great Mæcenas of his younger days, Lord Halifax, who had ventured some foolish criticisms on Pope's translation of the Iliad, and seems to have expected that the poet should dedicate the great work to him in return for an offer of a pension which he made and Pope declined. There is no reason to believe that Pope cherished any very bitter resentment toward Halifax. On the contrary, in a poem published some years after the Epistle he boasted of his friendship with Halifax, naming him outright, and adding in a note that the noble lord was no less distinguished by his love of letters than his abilities in Parliament.

The third passage, a tender reference to his mother's age and weakness, was written at least as early as 1731, — Mrs. Pope died in 1733, — and was incorporated in the Epistle to round it off with a picture of the poet absorbed in his filial duties at the very time that Hervey and Lady Mary were heaping abuse upon him, as a monster devoid of all good qualities. And now having discussed the various insertions in the Epistle, let us look for a moment at the poem as a whole, and see what is the nature of Pope's defense of himself and of his reply to his enemies.

It is cast in the form of a dialogue between the poet himself and Arbuthnot. Pope begins by complaining of the misfortunes which his reputation as a successful man of letters has brought upon him. He is a mark for all the starving scribblers of the town who besiege him for advice, recommendations, and hard cash. Is it not enough to make a man write Dunciads? Arbuthnot warns him against the danger of making foes (ll. 101- 104), but Pope replies that his flatterers are even more intolerable than his open enemies. And with a little outburst of impatience, such as we may well imagine him to have indulged in during his later years, he cries:

Why did I write? What sin to me unknown

Dipt me in ink, my parents' or my own?

and begins with l. 125 his poetical autobiography. He tells of his
first childish efforts, of poetry taken up "to help me thro' this long
disease my life," and then goes on to speak of the noble and
famous friends who had praised his early work and urged him to
try his fortune in the open field of letters. He speaks of his first
poems, the Pastorals and Windsor Forest, harmless as Hervey's
own verses, and tells how even then critics like Dennis fell foul of
him. Rival authors hated him, too, especially such pilfering bards
as Philips. This he could endure, but the coldness and even
jealousy of such a man as Addison — and here appears the famous
portrait of Atticus — was another matter, serious enough to draw
tears from all lovers of mankind.

Passing on (l. 213) to the days of his great success when his Homer
was the talk of the town, he asserts his ignorance of all the arts of
puffery and his independence of mutual admiration societies. He
left those who wished a patron to the tender mercies of Halifax,
who fed fat on flattery and repaid his flatterers merely with a good
word or a seat at his table. After all, the poet could afford to lose
the society of Bufo's toadies while such a friend as Gay was left
him (l. 254).

After an eloquent expression of his wish for independence (ll. 261-
270), he goes on to speak of the babbling friends who insist that he

is always meditating some new satire, and persist in recognizing some wretched poetaster's lampoon as his. And so by a natural transition Pope comes to speak of his own satiric poems and their aims. He says, and rightly, that he has never attacked virtue or innocence. He reserves his lash for those who trample on their neighbors and insult "fallen worth," for cold or treacherous friends, liars, and babbling blockheads. Let Sporus (Hervey) tremble (l. 303). Arbuthnot interposes herewith an ejaculation of contemptuous pity; is it really worth the poet's while to castigate such a slight thing as Hervey, that "mere white curd"? But Pope has suffered too much from Hervey's insolence to stay his hand, and he now proceeds to lay on the lash with equal fury and precision, drawing blood at every stroke, until we seem to see the wretched fop writhing and shrieking beneath the whip. And then with a magnificent transition he goes on (ll. 332-337) to draw a portrait of himself. Here, he says in effect, is the real man that Sporus has so maligned. The portrait is idealized, of course; one could hardly expect a poet speaking in his own defense in reply to venomous attacks to dissect his own character with the stern impartiality of the critics of the succeeding century, but it is in all essentials a portrait at once impressive and true.

Arbuthnot again interrupts (l. 358) to ask why he spares neither the poor nor the great in his satire, and Pope replies that he hates knaves in every rank of life. Yet by nature, he insists, he is of an easy temper, more readily deceived than angered, and in a long catalogue of instances he illustrates his own patience and good nature (ll. 366-385). It must be frankly confessed that these lines do not ring true. Pope might in the heat of argument convince himself that he was humble and slow to wrath, but he has never succeeded in convincing his readers.

With l. 382 Pope turns to the defense of his family, which, as we have seen, his enemies had abused as base and obscure. He draws a noble picture of his dead father, "by nature honest, by experience wise" simple, modest, and temperate, and passes to the description of himself watching over the last years of his old mother, his sole care to

Explore the thought, explain the asking eye

And keep a while one parent from the sky.

If the length of days which Heaven has promised those who honor father and mother fall to his lot, may Heaven preserve him such a friend as Arbuthnot to bless those days. And Arbuthnot closes the dialogue with a word which is meant, I think, to sum up the whole discussion and to pronounce the verdict that Pope's life had been good and honorable.

Whether that blessing1 be deny'd or giv'n,

Thus far was right, the rest belongs to Heav'n.

It seems hardly necessary to point out the merits of so patent a masterpiece as the Epistle to Arbuthnot. In order to enjoy it to the full, indeed, one must know something of the life of the author, of the circumstances under which it was written, and, in general, of the social and political life of the time. But even without this special knowledge no reader can fail to appreciate the marvelous ease, fluency, and poignancy of this admirable satire. There is nothing like it in our language except Pope's other satires, and of all his satires it is, by common consent, easily the first. It surpasses the satiric poetry of Dryden in pungency and depth of feeling as easily as it does that of Byron in polish and artistic restraint. Its range of tone is remarkable. At times it reads like glorified conversation, as in the opening lines; at times it flames and quivers with emotion, as in the assault on Hervey, or in the defense of his parents. Even in the limited field of satiric portraiture there is a wide difference between the manner in which Pope has drawn the portrait of Atticus and that of Sporus. The latter is a masterpiece of pure invective; no allowances are made, no lights relieve the darkness of the shadows, the portrait is frankly inhuman. It is the product of an unrestrained outburst of bitter passion. The portrait of Atticus, on the other hand, was, as we know, the work of years. It is the product not of an outburst of fury, but of a slowly growing and intense dislike, which, while recognizing the merits of its object, fastened with peculiar power upon his faults and weaknesses. The studious restraint which controls the satirist's hand makes it only the more effective. We know well enough that the portrait is not a fair one, but we are forced to remind ourselves of this at every step to avoid the spell which Pope's apparent impartiality casts over our judgments. The whole passage reads not so much like the heated plea of an advocate as the measured summing-up of a judge, and the last couplet falls on our ears with the inevitability of a final sentence. But the peculiar merit of the Epistle to Arbuthnot consists neither in the ease and polish of its style, nor in the vigor and effectiveness of its satire, but in the insight it gives us into the heart and mind of the poet himself. It presents an ideal picture of Pope, the man and the author, of his life, his friendships, his love of his parents, his literary relationships and aims. And it is quite futile to object, as some critics have done, that this picture is not exactly in accordance with the known facts of Pope's life. No great man can be tried and judged on the mere record of his acts. We must know the circumstances that shaped these, and the motives that inspired them. A man's ideals, if genuinely held and honestly followed, are perhaps even more valuable contributions to our final estimate of the man himself than all he did or left undone.

All I could never be,

All, men ignored in me,

This, I was worth to God, whose wheel the pitcher shaped.

And in the Epistle to Arbuthnot we recognize in Pope ideals of independence, of devotion to his art, of simple living, of loyal friendship, and of filial piety which shine in splendid contrast with the gross, servile, and cynically immoral tone of the age and society in which he lived.

Footnote 1:   i. e. the blessing of Arbuthnot's future companionship, for which Pope (l. 413) had just prayed.

return to footnote mark

line

referenc

e

meanin

g

Advertisement

Dr. John Arbuthnot, one of Pope's most intimate friends, had been physician to Queen Anne, and was a man of letters as well as a doctor. Arbuthnot, Pope, and Swift had combined to get out a volume of Miscellanies in 1737. His health was failing rapidly at this time, and he died a month or so after the appearance of this Epistle.

Epistle

1
John John Searle, Pope's faithful servant.

4
Bedlam a lunatic asylum in London in Pope's day. Notice how Pope mentions, in the same breath, Bedlam and Parnassus, the hill of the Muses which poets might well be supposed to haunt.

8
thickets the

groves surrounding Pope's villa.

Grot. see

Introduction [grotto]

10   the

chariot   the

coach in which Pope drove.

the

barge   the boat

in which Pope was rowed upon the Thames.

13   the

Mint   a

district in London where debtors were free from arrest. As they could not be arrested anywhere on Sunday, Pope represents them as taking that day to inflict their visits on him.

15   parson

probabl

y a certain Eusden, who had some pretensions to letters, but who ruined himself by drink.

17   clerk

a law

clerk.

18   engross

write

legal papers.

19-20   An

imaginary portrait of a mad poet who keeps on writing verses even in his cell in Bedlam. Pope may have been thinking of Lee, a dramatist of Dryden's day who was confined for a time in this asylum.

23   Arthur

Arthur Moore, a member of Parliament for some years and well known in London society. His "giddy son," James Moore, who took the name of Moore Smythe, dabbled in letters and was a bitter enemy of Pope.

25   Cornus

Robert Lord Walpole, whose wife deserted him in 1734. Horace Walpole speaks of her as half mad.

31   sped

done for.

40

Pope's counsel to delay the publication of the works read to him is borrowed from Horace: "nonumque prematur in annum" '(Ars Poetica, 388).'

41   Drury-

land like

Grub Street, a haunt of poor authors at this time.

43   before

Term ends   before

the season is over; that is, as soon as the poem is written.

48   a

Prologue   for a

play. Of course a prologue by the famous Mr. Pope would be of great value to a poor and unknown dramatist.

49   Pitholeon

n   the

name of a foolish poet mentioned by Horace. Pope uses it here for his enemy Welsted, mentioned in l. 373. — 'his Grace:' the title given a Duke in Great Britain. The Duke here referred to is said to be the Duke of Argyle, one of the most influential of the great Whig lords.

53   Curll

           a

notorious publisher of the day, and an enemy of Pope. The implication is that if Pope will not grant Pitholeon's request, the latter will accept Curll's invitation and concoct a new libel against the poet.

60   Pope

was one of the few men of letters of his day who had not written a play, and he was at this time on bad terms with certain actors.

62   Bernard

Lintot, the publisher of Pope's translation of Homer.

66   go
snacks   share
the profits. Pope represents the unknown dramatist as trying to bribe him to give a favorable report of the play.

69   Midas

           an old

legend tells us that Midas was presented with a pair of ass's ears by an angry god whose music he had slighted. His barber, or, Chaucer says, his queen, discovered the change which Midas had tried to conceal, and unable to keep the secret whispered it to the reeds in the river, who straightway spread the news abroad.

75   With this line Arbuthnot is supposed to take up the conversation. This is indicated here and elsewhere by the letter A.

79   Dunciad see Introduction

85   Codrus a name borrowed from Juvenal to denote a foolish poet. Pope uses it here for some conceited dramatist who thinks none the less of himself because his tragedy is rejected with shouts of laughter.

96   Explain the exact meaning of this line.

97   Bavius a stock name for a bad poet. See note on Essay on Criticism, l. 34.

98   Philips Ambrose Philips, author among other things of a set of Pastorals that appeared in the same volume with Pope, 1709. Pope and he soon became bitter enemies. He was patronized by a Bishop Boulter.

99   Sappho

Here as
elsewhere Pope uses the name of the Greek poetess for his enemy,
Lady Mary Wortley Montague.

109

Grubstr
eet
a
wretched street in London, inhabited in Pope's day by hack writers,
most of whom were his enemies.

111

Curll
(see
note to l. 53) had printed a number of Pope's letters without the
poet's consent some years before this poem was written.

113-32

Pope
here describes the flatterers who were foolish enough to pay him
personal compliments. They compare him to Horace who was
short like Pope, though fat, and who seems to have suffered from
colds; also to Alexander, one of whose shoulders was higher than
the other, and to Ovid, whose other name, Naso, might indicate
that long noses were a characteristic feature of his family. Pope
really had large and beautiful eyes. Maro, l. 122, is Virgil.

123

With
this line Pope begins an account of his life as a poet. For his
precocity, see Introduction.

129

ease
amuse,
entertain.

'friend,

not Wife:'   the
reference is, perhaps, to Martha Blount, Pope's friend, and may
have been meant as a contradiction of his reported secret marriage
to her.

132   to bear
to

endure the pains and troubles of an invalid's life.

133

Granvill
e   George
Granville, Lord Lansdowne, a poet and patron of letters to whom
Pope had dedicated his Windsor Forest.

134   Walsh
see note

on Essay on Criticism, l. 729.

135   Garth
Sir

Samuel Garth, like Arbuthnot, a doctor, a man of letters, and an
early friend of Pope.

137

Charles
Talbot, Duke of Shrewsbury; John, Lord Somers; and John
Sheffield, Duke of Buckingham; all leading statesmen and patrons
of literature in Queen Anne's day.

138

Rochest
er   Francis
Atterbury, Bishop of Rochester, an intimate friend of Pope.

139   St. John

Bolingb
roke. For Pope's relations with him, see introduction to the Essay on Man, p. 116.

143

Gilbert
Burnet and John Oldmixon had written historical works from the Whig point of view. Roger Cooke, a now forgotten writer, had published a Detection of the Court and State of England. Pope in a note on this line calls them all three authors of secret and scandalous history.

146   The
reference is to Pope's early descriptive poems, the Pastorals and Windsor Forest.

147   gentle
Fanny's   a sneer
at Lord Hervey's verses. See the introduction to this poem.

149   Gildon
a critic
of the time who had repeatedly attacked Pope. The poet told Spence that he had heard Addison gave Gildon ten pounds to slander him.

151   Dennis
see note
on Essay on Criticism. l. 270.

156   kiss'd
the rod   Pope
was sensible enough to profit by the criticisms even of his enemies. He corrected several passages in the Essay on Criticism which Dennis had properly found fault with.

162   **Bentley** the

most famous scholar of Pope's day. Pope disliked him because of his criticism of the poet's translation of the Iliad, "good verses, but not Homer." The epithet "slashing" refers to Bentley's edition of Paradise Lost in which he altered and corrected the poet's text to suit his own ideas.

Tibbald

s   **Lewis**

Theobald (pronounced Tibbald), a scholar who had attacked Pope's edition of Shakespeare. Pope calls him "piddling" because of his scrupulous attention to details.

177   the

Bard   **Philips,**

see note on l. 98. Pope claimed that Philips's Pastorals were plagiarized from Spenser, and other poets. Philips, also, translated some Persian Tales for the low figure of half a crown apiece.

187   **bade**

translate

suggest

ed that they translate other men's work, since they could write nothing valuable of their own.

188   **Tate**

a

poetaster of the generation before Pope. He is remembered as the part author of a doggerel version of the Psalms.

191-212   **For**

a discussion of this famous passage, see introduction to the Epistle.

196   the

Turk   it was
formerly the practice for a Turkish monarch when succeeding to
the throne to have all his brothers murdered so as to do away with
possible rivals.

199   faint
praise
                                                             Addiso
n was hearty enough when he cared to praise his friends. Pope is
thinking of the coldness with which Addison treated his Pastorals
as compared to those of Philips.

206   oblig'd
                                                             note the
old-fashioned pronunciation to rhyme with "besieged."

207   Cato
                                                             an
unmistakable allusion to Addison's tragedy in which the famous
Roman appears laying down the law to the remnants of the Senate.

209
                                                             Templa
rs   students
of law at the "Temple" in London who prided themselves on their
good taste in literature. A body of them came on purpose to
applaud 'Cato' on the first night.

                                                             raise
                                                             exalt,
praise.

211-2   laugh ...
weep   explain
the reason for these actions.

Atticus
Addiso

n's name was given in the first version of this passage. Then it was changed to "A — -n." Addison had been mentioned in the Spectator (No. 150) under the name of Atticus as "in every way one of the greatest geniuses the age has produced."

213   rubric
on the walls   Lintot,
Pope's old publisher, used to stick up the titles of new books in red letters on the walls of his shop.

214   with
claps   with
clap-bills, posters.

215

                                                           smokin
g   hot
from the press.

220   George
                                                           George
II, king of England at this time. His indifference to literature was notorious.

228   Bufo
                                                           the
picture of a proud but grudging patron of letters which follows was first meant for Bubb Doddington, a courtier and patron of letters at the time the poem was written. In order to connect it more closely with the time of which he was writing, Pope added ll. 243-246, which pointed to Charles Montague, Earl of Halifax. Halifax was himself a poet and affected to be a great patron of poetry, but his enemies accused him of only giving his clients "good words and

good dinners." Pope tells an amusing story of Montague's comments on his translation of the Iliad (Spence, Anecdotes, p. 134). But Halifax subscribed for ten copies of the translation, so that Pope, at least, could not complain of his lack of generosity.

Castalian state the
kingdom of poets

232 His
name was coupled with that of Horace as a poet and critic.

234 Pindar
without a head some
headless statue which Bufo insisted was a genuine classic figure of Pindar, the famous Greek lyric poet.

237 his seat
his
country seat.

242 paid in
kind What
does this phrase mean?

243
Dryden
died in 1700. He had been poor and obliged to work hard for a living in his last years, but hardly had to starve. Halifax offered to pay the expenses of his funeral and contribute five hundred pounds for a monument, and Pope not unreasonably suggests that some of this bounty might have been bestowed on Dryden in his lifetime.

249
When a
politician wants a writer to put in a day's work in defending him.

Walpole, for example, who cared nothing for poetry, spent large sums in retaining writers to defend him in the journals and pamphlets of the day.

254   John
Gay, the author of some very entertaining verses, was an intimate friend of Pope. On account of some supposed satirical allusions his opera Polly was refused a license, and when his friends, the Duke and Duchess of Queensberry (see l. 260) solicited subscriptions for it in the palace, they were driven from the court. Gay died in 1732, and Pope wrote an epitaph for his tomb in Westminster Abbey. It is to this that he alludes in l. 258.

274   Balbus
                                                                     Balbus
is said to mean the Earl of Kinnoul, at one time an acquaintance of Pope and Swift.

278   Sir
William Yonge, a Whig politician whom Pope disliked. He seems to have written occasional verses. Bubo is Bubo Doddington (see note on l 230).

297-8   In
the Fourth Moral Essay, published in 1731 as an Epistle to the Earl of Burlington, Pope had given a satirical description of a nobleman's house and grounds, adorned and laid out at vast expense, but in bad taste. Certain features of this description were taken from Canons, the splendid country place of the Duke of Chandos, and the duke was at once identified by a scandal-loving public with the Timon of the poem. In the description Pope speaks of the silver bell which calls worshipers to Timon's chapel, and of the soft Dean preaching there "who never mentions Hell to ears polite." In this passage of the Epistle to Arbuthnot he is protesting

against the people who swore that they could identify the bell and the Dean as belonging to the chapel at Canons.

303   Sporus
a
favorite of Nero, used here for Lord Hervey. See introduction to this poem.

304   ass's
milk   Hervey
was obliged by bad health to keep a strict diet, and a cup of ass's milk was his daily drink.

308   painted
child   Hervey
was accustomed to paint his face like a woman.

317-9
                                                       Pope is
thinking of Milton's striking description of Satan "squat like a toad" by the ear of the sleeping Eve (Paradise Lost, IV, 800). In this passage "Eve" refers to Queen Caroline with whom Hervey was on intimate terms. It is said that he used to have a seat in the queen's hunting chaise "where he sat close behind her perched at her ear".

322   now
master up, now miss   Pope
borrowed this telling phrase from a pamphlet against Hervey written by Pulteney, a political opponent, in which the former is called "a pretty little master-miss."

326   the
board   the
Council board where Hervey sat as member of the Privy Council.

328-9   An
allusion to the old pictures of the serpent in Eden with a snake's
body and a woman's, or angel's, face.

330   parts
         talents,
natural gifts.

338-9   An
allusion to Pope's abandoning the imaginative topics to his early
poems, as the Pastorals and The Rape of the Lock, and turning to
didactic verse as in the Essay on Man, and the Moral Epistles.

347   An
allusion to a story circulated, in an abusive pamphlet called A Pop
upon Pope, that the poet had been whipped for his satire and that
he had cried like a child.

349   Dull
and scandalous poems printed under Pope's name, or attributed to
him by his enemies.

351   the
pictur'd shape   Pope
was especially hurt by the caricatures which exaggerated his
personal deformity.

353   a friend
is exile

         probabl
y Bishop Atterbury, then in exile for his Jacobite opinions.

354-5

         Another
reference to Hervey who was suspected of poisoning the mind of
the King against Pope.

361   Japhet

Japhet
Crooke, a notorious forger of the time. He died in prison in 1734,
after having had his nose slit and ears cropped for his crimes; see
below, l. 365.

363   Knight
of the post   a slang
term for a professional witness ready to, swear to anything for
money. A knight of the shire, on the other hand, is the
representative of a county in the House of Commons.

367   bit
tricked,
taken in, a piece of Queen Anne slang. The allusion is probably to
the way in which Lady Mary Wortley Montague allowed Pope to
make love to her and then laughed at him.

369   friend
to his distress   in 1733,
when old Dennis was in great poverty, a play was performed for
his benefit, for which Pope obligingly wrote a prologue.

371

Colley
Gibber, actor and poet laureate. Pope speaks as if it were an act of
condescension for him to have drunk with Gibber."

Moore
James
Moore Smythe (see note on l. 23), whom Pope used to meet at the
house of the Blounts. He wrote a comedy, The Rival Modes, in
which he introduced six lines that Pope had written. Pope
apparently had given him leave to do so, and then retracted his
permission. But Moore used them without the permission and an

undignified quarrel arose as to the true authorship of the passage.

373   Welsted
                                                                      a hack
writer of the day, had falsely charged Pope with being responsible
for the death of the lady who is celebrated in Pope's Elegy to the
Memory of an Unfortunate Lady.

374-5
                                                                 There is
an allusion here that has never been fully explained. Possibly the
passage refers to Teresa Blount whom Pope suspected of having
circulated slanderous reports concerning his relations with her
sister.

376-7
                                                                  Suffere
d Budgell to attribute to his (Pope's) pen the slanderous gossip of
the Grub Street Journal, — a paper to which Pope did, as a matter
of fact, contribute — and let him (Budgell) write anything he
pleased except his (Pope's) will. Budgell, a distant cousin of
Addison's, fell into bad habits after his friend's death. He was
strongly suspected of having forged a will by which Dr. Tindal of
Oxford left him a considerable sum of money. He finally drowned
himself in the Thames.

378   the two
Curlls   Curll,
the bookseller, and Lord Hervey whom Pope here couples with
him because of Hervey's vulgar abuse of Pope's personal
deformities and obscure parentage.

380   yet why
                                                                      Why
should they abuse Pope's inoffensive parents? Compare the

following lines.

383

Moore's

own mother was suspected of loose conduct.

386-8 Of
gentle blood ... each parent Pope
asserted, perhaps incorrectly, that his father belonged to a
gentleman's family, the head of which was the Earl of Downe. His
mother was the daughter of a Yorkshire gentleman, who lost two
sons in the service of Charles I (cf. l. 386).

389 Bestia
probabl
y the elder Horace Walpole, who was in receipt of a handsome
pension.

391 An
allusion to Addison's unhappy marriage with the Countess of
Warwick.

393 the
good man Pope's
father, who as a devout Roman Catholic refused to take the oath of
allegiance (cf. l. 395), or risk the equivocations sanctioned by the
"schoolmen," i.e. the Catholic casuists of the day (l. 398).

404 friend
Arbuthn
ot, to whom the epistle is addressed.

405-11 The
first draft of these appeared in a letter to Aaron Hill, September 3,
1731, where Pope speaks of having sent them "the other day to a
particular friend," perhaps the poet Thomson. Mrs. Pope, who was

very old and feeble, was of course alive when they were first written, but died more than a year before the passage appeared in its revised form in this Epistle.

412   An allusion to the promise contained in the fifth commandment.

415   served a Queen

                                                                      Arbuthn ot had been Queen Anne's doctor, but was driven out of his rooms in the palace after her death.

416   that blessing   long life for Arbuthnot. It was, in fact, denied, for he died a month or so after the appearance of the Epistle.

Contents

Notes on An Ode on Solitude

Pope says that this delightful little poem was written at the early age of twelve. It first appeared in a letter to his friend, Henry Cromwell, dated July 17, 1709. There are several variations between this first form and that in which it was finally published, and it is probable that Pope thought enough of his boyish production to subject it to repeated revision. Its spirit is characteristic of a side of Pope's nature that is often forgotten. He was, indeed, the poet of the society of his day, urban, cultured, and pleasure-loving; but to the end of his days he retained a love for the quiet charm of country life which he had come to feel in his boyhood at Binfield, and for which he early withdrew from the whirl and dissipations of London to the groves and the grotto of his villa at Twickenham.

Contents / Contents, p. 2

Notes on The Descent of Dullness

In the fourth book of the Dunciad, Pope abandons the satire on the pretenders to literary fame which had run through the earlier books, and flies at higher game. He represents the Goddess Dullness as "coming in her majesty to destroy Order and Science, and to substitute the Kingdom of the Dull upon earth." He attacks the pedantry and formalism of university education in his day, the dissipation and false taste of the traveled gentry, the foolish pretensions to learning of collectors and virtuosi, and the daringly irreverent speculations of freethinkers and infidels. At the close of the book he represents the Goddess as dismissing her worshipers with a speech which she concludes with "a yawn of extraordinary virtue." Under its influence "all nature nods," and pulpits, colleges, and Parliament succumb. The poem closes with the magnificent description of the descent of Dullness and her final conquest of art, philosophy, and religion. It is said that Pope himself admired these lines so much that he could not repeat them without his voice faltering with emotion. "And well it might, sir," said Dr. Johnson when this anecdote was repeated to him, "for they are noble lines." And Thackeray in his lecture on Pope in The English Humorists says:

"In these astonishing lines Pope reaches, I think, to the very greatest height which his sublime art has attained, and shows himself the equal of all poets of all times. It is the brightest ardor, the loftiest assertion of truth, the most generous wisdom, illustrated by the noblest poetic figure, and spoken in words the aptest, grandest, and most harmonious."

Contents / Contents, p. 2

Notes on The Epitaph on Gay

John Gay, the idlest, best-natured, and best-loved man of letters of his day, was the special friend of Pope. His early work, The Shepherd's Week, was planned as a parody on the Pastorals of Pope's rival, Ambrose Philips, and Pope assisted him in the composition of his luckless farce, Three Hours after Marriage. When Gay's opera Polly was forbidden by the licenser, and Gay's patrons, the Duke and Duchess of Queensberry, were driven from court for soliciting subscriptions for him, Pope warmly espoused his cause. Gay died in 1732 and was buried in Westminster Abbey. Pope's epitaph for his tomb was first published in the quarto edition of Pope's works in 1735 — Johnson, in his discussion of Pope's epitaphs (Lives of the Poets), devotes a couple of pages of somewhat captious criticism to these lines; but they have at least the virtue of simplicity and sincerity, and are at once an admirable portrait of the man and a lasting tribute to the poet Gay.

Contents /

Appendix

The Rape of the Lock: First Edition

Nolueram, Belinda, tuos violare capillos

Sed juvat, hoc precibus me tribuisse tuis.

Mart.

Canto I

What dire offence from am'rous causes springs,

What mighty quarrels rise from trivial things,

I sing — This verse to C — l, Muse! is due:

This, ev'n Belinda may vouchsafe to view:

Slight is the subject, but not so the praise,

If she inspire, and he approve my lays.

Say what strange motive, goddess! could compel

A well-bred lord t' assault a gentle belle?

O say what stranger cause, yet unexplored,

Could make a gentle belle reject a lord?

And dwells such rage in softest bosoms then,

And lodge such daring souls in little men?

Sol through white curtains did his beams display,

And ope'd those eyes which brighter shine than they,

Shock just had giv'n himself the rousing shake,

And nymphs prepared their chocolate to take;

Thrice the wrought slipper knocked against the ground,

And striking watches the tenth hour resound.

Belinda rose, and midst attending dames,

Launched on the bosom of the silver Thames:

A train of well-dressed youths around her shone,

And ev'ry eye was fixed on her alone:

On her white breast a sparkling cross she wore

Which Jews might kiss and infidels adore.

Her lively looks a sprightly mind disclose,

Quick as her eyes, and as unfixed as those:

Favours to none, to all she smiles extends;

Oft she rejects, but never once offends.

Bright as the sun, her eyes the gazers strike,

And, like the sun, they shine on all alike.

Yet graceful ease, and sweetness void of pride,

Might hide her faults, if belles had faults to hide:

If to her share some female errors fall,

Look on her face, and you'll forgive 'em all.

This nymph, to the destruction of mankind,

Nourished two locks, which graceful hung behind

In equal curls, and well conspired to deck

With shining ringlets her smooth iv'ry neck.

Love in these labyrinths his slaves detains,

And mighty hearts are held in slender chains.

With hairy springes we the birds betray,

Slight lines of hair surprise the finny prey,

Fair tresses man's imperial race insnare,

And beauty draws us with a single hair.

Th' adventurous baron the bright locks admired;

He saw, he wished, and to the prize aspired.

Resolved to win, he meditates the way,

By force to ravish, or by fraud betray;

For when success a lover's toil attends,

Few ask if fraud or force attained his ends.

For this, ere Phoebus rose, he had implored

Propitious heav'n, and every pow'r adored,

But chiefly Love — to Love an altar built,

Of twelve vast French romances, neatly gilt.

There lay the sword-knot Sylvia's hands had sewn

With Flavia's busk that oft had wrapped his own:

A fan, a garter, half a pair of gloves,

And all the trophies of his former loves.

With tender billets-doux he lights the pire,

And breathes three am'rous sighs to raise the fire.

Then prostrate falls, and begs with ardent eyes

Soon to obtain, and long possess the prize:

The pow'rs gave ear, and granted half his pray'r,

The rest the winds dispersed in empty air.

Close by those meads, for ever crowned with flow'rs,

Where Thames with pride surveys his rising tow'rs,

There stands a structure of majestic frame,

Which from the neighb'ring Hampton takes its name.

Here Britain's statesmen oft the fall foredoom

Of foreign tyrants, and of nymphs at home;

Here thou, great Anna! whom three realms obey,

Dost sometimes counsel take — and sometimes tea.

Hither our nymphs and heroes did resort,

To taste awhile the pleasures of a court;

In various talk the cheerful hours they passed,

Of who was bit, or who capotted last;

This speaks the glory of the British queen,

And that describes a charming Indian screen;

A third interprets motions, looks, and eyes;

At ev'ry word a reputation dies.

Snuff, or the fan, supply each pause of chat,

With singing, laughing, ogling, and all that.

Now when, declining from the noon of day,

The sun obliquely shoots his burning ray;

When hungry judges soon the sentence sign,

And wretches hang that jurymen may dine;

When merchants from th' Exchange return in peace,

And the long labours of the toilet cease,

The board's with cups and spoons, alternate, crowned,

The berries crackle, and the mill turns round;

On shining altars of Japan they raise

The silver lamp, and fiery spirits blaze:

From silver spouts the grateful liquors glide,

While China's earth receives the smoking tide.

At once they gratify their smell and taste,

While frequent cups prolong the rich repast.

Coffee (which makes the politician wise,

And see through all things with his half-shut eyes)

Sent up in vapours to the baron's brain

New stratagems, the radiant lock to gain.

Ah cease, rash youth! desist ere't is too late,

Fear the just gods, and think of Scylla's fate!

Changed to a bird, and sent to flit in air,

She dearly pays for Nisus' injured hair!

But when to mischief mortals bend their mind,

How soon fit instruments of ill they find!

Just then, Clarissa drew with tempting grace

A two-edged weapon from her shining case:

So ladies, in romance, assist their knight,

Present the spear, and arm him for the fight;

He takes the gift with rev'rence, and extends

The little engine on his fingers' ends;

This just behind Belinda's neck he spread,

As o'er the fragrant steams she bends her head.

He first expands the glitt'ring forfex wide

T' enclose the lock; then joins it, to divide;

One fatal stroke the sacred hair does sever

From the fair head, for ever, and for ever!

The living fires come flashing from her eyes,

And screams of horror rend th' affrighted skies.

Not louder shrieks by dames to heav'n are cast,

When husbands die, or lapdogs breathe their last;

Or when rich china vessels, fall'n from high,

In glitt'ring dust and painted fragments lie!

"Let wreaths of triumph now my temples twine,"

The victor cried, "the glorious prize is mine!

While fish in streams, or birds delight in air,

Or in a coach and six the British fair,

As long as Atalantis shall be read,

Or the small pillow grace a lady's bed,

While visits shall be paid on solemn days,

When num'rous wax-lights in bright order blaze,

While nymphs take treats, or assignations give,

So long my honour, name, and praise shall live!"

What time would spare, from steel receives its date,

And monuments, like men, submit to fate!

Steel did the labour of the gods destroy,

And strike to dust th' aspiring tow'rs of Troy;

Steel could the works of mortal pride confound,

And hew triumphal arches to the ground.

What wonder then, fair nymph! thy hairs should feel

The conqu'ring force of unresisted steel?

5

10

15

20

25

30

35

40

45

50

55

60

65

70

75

80

85

90

95

100

105

110

115

120

125

130

135

140

Canto II

But anxious cares the pensive nymph oppressed,

And secret passions laboured in her breast.

Not youthful kings in battle seized alive,

Not scornful virgins who their charms survive,

Not ardent lover robbed of all his bliss,

Not ancient lady when refused a kiss,

Not tyrants fierce that unrepenting die,

Not Cynthia when her manteau's pinned awry,

E'er felt such rage, resentment, and despair,

As thou, sad virgin! for thy ravished hair.

While her racked soul repose and peace requires,

The fierce Thalestris fans the rising fires.

"O wretched maid!" she spread her hands, and cried,

(And Hampton's echoes, "Wretched maid!" replied)

"Was it for this you took such constant care

Combs, bodkins, leads, pomatums to prepare?

For this your locks in paper durance bound?

For this with tort'ring irons wreathed around?

Oh had the youth been but content to seize

Hairs less in sight, or any hairs but these!

Gods! shall the ravisher display this hair,

While the fops envy, and the ladies stare!

Honour forbid! at whose unrivalled shrine

Ease, pleasure, virtue, all, our sex resign.

Methinks already I your tears survey,

Already hear the horrid things they say,

Already see you a degraded toast,

And all your honour in a whisper lost!

How shall I, then, your helpless fame defend?

'T will then be infamy to seem your friend!

And shall this prize, th' inestimable prize,

Exposed through crystal to the gazing eyes,

And heightened by the diamond's circling rays,

On that rapacious hand for ever blaze?

Sooner shall grass in Hyde Park Circus grow,

And wits take lodgings in the sound of Bow;

Sooner let earth, air, sea, to chaos fall,

Men, monkeys, lapdogs, parrots, perish all!"

She said; then raging to Sir Plume repairs,

And bids her beau demand the precious hairs:

Sir Plume, of amber snuff-box justly vain,

And the nice conduct of a clouded cane,

With earnest eyes, and round unthinking face,

He first the snuff-box opened, then the case,

And thus broke out — "My lord, why, what the devil!

Zounds! damn the lock! 'fore Gad, you must be civil!

Plague on't! 't is past a jest — nay, prithee, pox!

Give her the hair." — He spoke, and rapped his box.

"It grieves me much," replied the peer again,

"Who speaks so well should ever speak in vain:

But by this lock, this sacred lock, I swear,

(Which never more shall join its parted hair;

Which never more its honours shall renew,

Clipped from the lovely head where once it grew)

That, while my nostrils draw the vital air,

This hand, which won it, shall for ever wear."

He spoke, and speaking, in proud triumph spread

The long-contended honours of her head.

But see! the nymph in sorrow's pomp appears,

Her eyes half-languishing, half drowned in tears;

Now livid pale her cheeks, now glowing red

On her heaved bosom hung her drooping head,

Which with a sigh she raised, and thus she said:

"For ever cursed be this detested day,

Which snatched my best, my fav'rite curl away;

Happy! ah ten times happy had I been,

If Hampton Court these eyes had never seen!

Yet am not I the first mistaken maid,

By love of courts to num'rous ills betrayed.

O had I rather unadmired remained

In some lone isle, or distant northern land,

Where the gilt chariot never marked the way,

Where none learn ombre, none e'er taste bohea!

There kept my charms concealed from mortal eye,

Like roses, that in deserts bloom and die.

What moved my mind with youthful lords to roam?

O had I stayed, and said my pray'rs at home!

'Twas this the morning omens did foretell,

Thrice from my trembling hand the patchbox fell;

The tott'ring china shook without a wind,

Nay, Poll sat mute, and Shock was most unkind!

See the poor remnants of this slighted hair!

My hands shall rend what ev'n thy own did spare:

This in two sable ringlets taught to break,

Once gave new beauties to the snowy neck;

The sister-lock now sits uncouth, alone,

And in its fellow's fate foresees its own;

Uncurled it hangs, the fatal shears demands,

And tempts once more thy sacrilegious hands."

She said: the pitying audience melt in tears;

But fate and Jove had stopped the baron's ears.

In vain Thalestris with reproach assails,

For who can move when fair Belinda fails?

Not half so fixed the Trojan could remain,

While Anna begged and Dido raged in vain.

"To arms, to arms!" the bold Thalestris cries,

And swift as lightning to the combat flies.

All side in parties, and begin th' attack;

Fans clap, silks rustle, and tough whalebones crack;

Heroes' and heroines' shouts confus'dly rise,

And bass and treble voices strike the skies;

No common weapons in their hands are found,

Like gods they fight, nor dread a mortal wound.

So when bold Homer makes the gods engage,

And heav'nly breasts with human passions rage,

'Gainst Pallas, Mars; Latona, Hermes arms,

And all Olympus rings with loud alarms;

Jove's thunder roars, heav'n trembles all around,

Blue Neptune storms, the bellowing deeps resound:

Earth shakes her nodding tow'rs, the ground gives way,

And the pale ghosts start at the flash of day!

While through the press enraged Thalestris flies,

And scatters death around from both her eyes,

A beau and witling perished in the throng,

One died in metaphor, and one in song.

"O cruel nymph; a living death I bear,"

Cried Dapperwit, and sunk beside his chair.

A mournful glance Sir Fopling upwards cast,

"Those eyes are made so killing" — was his last.

Thus on Mæander's flow'ry margin lies

Th' expiring swan, and as he sings he dies.

As bold Sir Plume had drawn Clarissa down,

Chloe stepped in, and killed him with a frown;

She smiled to see the doughty hero slain,

But at her smile the beau revived again.

Now Jove suspends his golden scales in air,

Weighs the men's wits against the lady's hair;

The doubtful beam long nods from side to side;

At length the wits mount up, the hairs subside.

See fierce Belinda on the baron flies,

With more than usual lightning in her eyes:

Nor feared the chief th' unequal fight to try,

Who sought no more than on his foe to die.

But this bold lord, with manly strength endued,

She with one finger and a thumb subdued:

Just where the breath of life his nostrils drew,

A charge of snuff the wily virgin threw;

Sudden, with starting tears each eye o'erflows,

And the high dome re-echoes to his nose.

"Now meet thy fate," th' incensed virago cried,

And drew a deadly bodkin from her side.

"Boast not my fall," he said, "insulting foe!

Thou by some other shalt be laid as low;

Nor think to die dejects my lofty mind;

All that I dread is leaving you behind!

Rather than so, ah let me still survive,

And still burn on, in Cupid's flames, alive."

"Restore the lock!" she cries; and all around

"Restore the lock!" the vaulted roofs rebound.

Not fierce Othello in so loud a strain

Roared for the handkerchief that caused his pain.

But see how oft ambitious aims are crossed,

And chiefs contend till all the prize is lost!

The lock, obtained with guilt, and kept with pain,

In ev'ry place is sought, but sought in vain:

With such a prize no mortal must be blessed,

So heav'n decrees! with heav'n who can contest?

Some thought it mounted to the lunar sphere,

Since all that man e'er lost is treasured there.

There heroes' wits are kept in pond'rous vases,

And beaux' in snuff-boxes and tweezer-cases.

There broken vows, and death-bed alms are found,

And lovers' hearts with ends of ribbon bound,

The courtier's promises, and sick man's pray'rs,

The smiles of harlots, and the tears of heirs,

Cages for gnats, and chains to yoke a flea,

Dried butterflies, and tomes of casuistry.

But trust the muse — she saw it upward rise,

Though marked by none but quick poetic eyes:

(Thus Rome's great founder to the heav'ns withdrew,

To Proculus alone confessed in view)

A sudden star, it shot through liquid air,

And drew behind a radiant trail of hair.

Not Berenice's locks first rose so bright,

The skies bespangling with dishevelled light.

(This the beau monde shall from the Mall survey,

(As through the moonlight shade they nightly stray,

(And hail with music its propitious ray;

This Partridge soon shall view in cloudless skies,

When next he looks through Galileo's eyes;

And hence th' egregious wizard shall foredoom

The fate of Louis, and the fall of Rome.

Then cease, bright nymph! to mourn thy ravished hair,

Which adds new glory to the shining sphere!

Not all the tresses that fair head can boast,

Shall draw such envy as the lock you lost.

For after all the murders of your eye,

When, after millions slain, yourself shall die;

When those fair suns shall set, as set they must,

And all those tresses shall be laid in dust,

This lock the muse shall consecrate to fame,

And 'midst the stars inscribe Belinda's name.

5

10

15

20

25

30

35

40

45

50

55

60

65

70

75

80

85

90

95

100

105

110

115

120

125

130

135

140

145

150

155

160

165

170

175

180

185

190

Contents / Contents, p. 2

end of text

CPSIA information can be obtained
at www.ICGtesting.com
Printed in the USA
LVHW022347050922
727595LV00008B/148